STUDIES FROM AN EASTERN HOME

STUDIES FROM AN EASTERN HOME

SISTER NIVEDITA

GYAN

Published by

Gyan Publishing House
5, Ansari Road
Daryaganj, New Delhi-110002
Phone: 011-47034999, 9811692060
E-mail: books@gyanbooks.com

Distribution Network
gyanbooks.com
India, USA, Canada, UK, Australia

ISBN: 978-93-6920-104-4 (PB)

First Published, 1913

2nd Impression 2025

Printed at: Gyan Press, Delhi.

STUDIES FROM AN EASTERN HOME
Author: SISTER NIVEDITA

STUDIES FROM AN EASTERN HOME

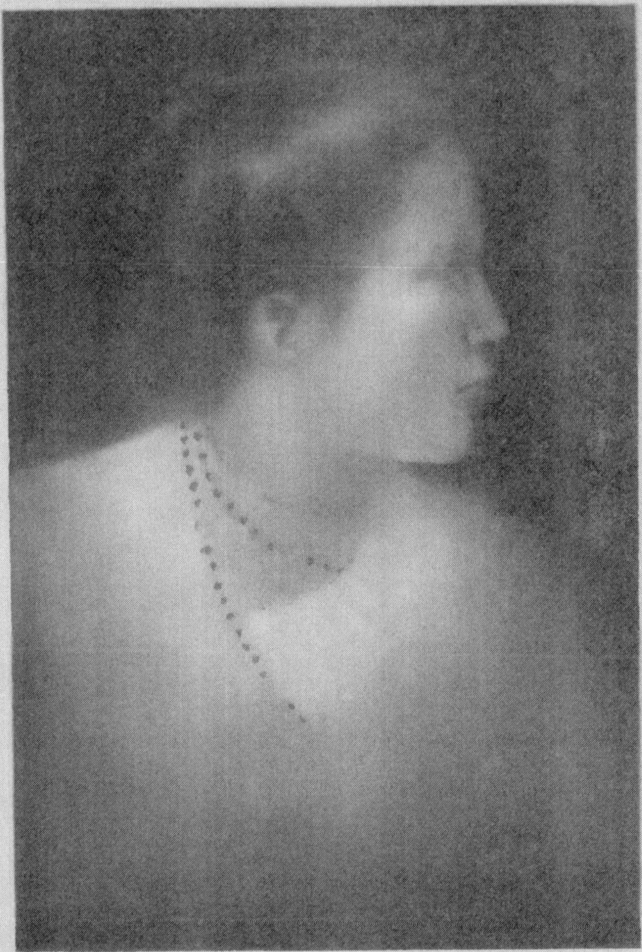

SISTER NIVEDITA (MARGARET E. NOBLE)

STUDIES FROM AN EASTERN HOME

BY

THE SISTER NIVEDITA

(MARGARET E. NOBLE)

AUTHOR OF "THE WEB OF INDIAN LIFE," "THE MASTER AS I SAW HIM," ETC.

LONGMANS, GREEN AND CO.

39 PATERNOSTER ROW, LONDON

NEW YORK, BOMBAY, AND CALCUTTA

1913

CONTENTS

MARGARET NOBLE:

IN MEMORIAM

IT is now nearly ten years since there was published, under the title of *The Web of Indian Life*, a book which immediately found its appropriate public. In England and America it was recognised as belonging to that newer and finer type of interpretation as applied to the East of which our time has produced some noteworthy examples; in India it was welcomed as almost the first attempt on the part of an English writer to present the ethical and social ideals embodied in the Indian woman and family. Many among the readers of the book were aware that its author stood in a unique relation to the Indian people: that she had identified herself without reserve with their life and been dedicated wholly to their service; while not a few were assured that she was destined to carry forward the task thus brilliantly begun of revealing the inner side of Eastern society to the West. But this was not to be. Two years ago she died, with her work in India, as it seemed to those who knew her best and had most reason to hope greatly, hardly more than envisaged and planned.

Margaret Noble, known for some twelve years to multitudes of people throughout India as Sister Nivedita, was of Irish parentage and birth, and was born at Dungannon, Co. Tyrone, in 1867. Very soon afterwards her father, Samuel Richmond Noble, entered the Lancashire Independent College, in preparation for the Congregational ministry, but did not live to fulfil his early promise. Margaret, his elder daughter, passed from school in the north of England to a teacher's training, and was fortunate enough to become acquainted in London with some of the most enthusiastic apostles of the New Education. Her practical experience was gained as teacher in various girls' schools, and more especially in association with a Dutch lady who had established in a suburb of South London a school of a thoroughly modern type. In 1892, being then in her twenty-fifth year, she opened at Wimbledon a school of her own in which she strove to give expression to the broad and fine conception of girls' education with which then and afterwards she was identified. At Wimbledon, too, she was the centre of a group of friends, eager inquirers into everything, given to the discussion of books, ethics, and society with the confident energy of youth, and beginning in several directions social work which has since borne varied fruit. Always, however, with Margaret Noble, intellectual inquiry was immediately related to what she regarded as her proper work—education; and she was one of the most active of those, mostly, like herself, concerned with the newer applications of educational theory, who, twenty years or so ago, founded the Sesame Club, the earliest in this country of those social centres for men and women which have since so largely multiplied.

Busy with her school and kindred schemes, abounding in life, a keen reader and thinker, with a continually widening circle of friends—such she was in 1895, when there came into her life the influence which in a few months altered its whole current and purpose.

It was, as she has recorded in *The Master as I Saw Him*, at a drawing-room meeting in November of the year just mentioned that Margaret Noble for the first time met the Swami Vivekananda, who had been recognised by many as a challenging figure in the London of that time. He had appeared before the Parliament of Religions, held during the Chicago Exhibition of 1893, as the first of the modern missionaries of Hinduism to the Western world. He was unknown and had come unheralded; but his discourse—the one incident of that curious assembly that is remembered to-day—was epoch-marking. From it must be dated the widespread interest in Indian thought and religion, and especially in the philosophy of Vedanta, which has been so unmistakable a feature of educated America during the past two decades.

You will hear from those who came within the scope of this masterful teacher's influence many differing estimates of the effect created by his personality and speech. Before leaving India, he had been known as the specially chosen disciple of Ramakrishna Paramahamsa, the Bengali saint who had lived in a temple-garden at Dakshineshwar, on the river a few miles above Calcutta, and whose life and sayings were made known to European readers through one of Max-Müller's later books. To Sister Nivedita herself the life lived by Ramakrishna and extended and interpreted by his chief follower summed up the Hindu consciousness, and stood for the final proof of "the entire sufficiency of any single creed or conception to lead the soul to God as its true goal."

> "Henceforth," she wrote, "it is not true that each form of life or worship is tolerated or understood by the Hindu mind: each form is justified, welcomed, set

> up for its passionate loving, for evermore. Henceforth, the supreme crime for any follower of any Indian sect, whether orthodox or modern, philosophic or popular, shall be the criticism of any other, as if it were without the bounds of the Eternal Faith."

But Ramakrishna was a pure devotee: his concern was simply the realisation in the individual of the Divine. Vivekananda was a man of action. Not only did he carry westward the message of Vedantism, but he had dreams of a renewal of the life of India through the infusion of fresh knowledge and renascent ideals. He stood entirely aloof from politics: yet it is hardly surprising that his younger followers should have acclaimed him as something more than a teacher of Vedantism—as, in truth, the prophet of New India in a sense which, it seems quite certain, he never for a moment intended.

The Swami left America for England in August 1895, and a few weeks later he had begun lecturing in London. Miss Noble had few opportunities of hearing him before his return to America during the winter, but in the spring of 1896 he was back in London, and was holding a class in the house of an English friend in St. George's Road, near Victoria Station. There she was a constant and for a time a hostile and contentious hearer. Always passionately religious, she had in her girlhood become a member of the Anglican Church and was deeply responsive to its ritual and sentiment. But the doctrines of orthodoxy had long since ceased to hold her intelligence; and at twenty-eight, in the full tide of her manifold intellectual interests, she was, it may be supposed, as completely detached from the religious beliefs of her childhood as from the occult ideas by which at that time some among her friends were impressed. The message of Swami Vivekananda went to the mark, little as she recognised this at the time. She disputed his assertions, fought him in the discussion class, provided indeed the strongest antagonism which he had to meet at any of his London gatherings. But it is clear that from the first his influence was winning. About his teaching there was nothing that could be associated with any sect or special doctrine. Although himself obeying the impulse and fulfilling the purpose of his master Ramakrishna, he dealt always impersonally with the body of truth common to all religions, and dwelt upon the necessity, especially in the present stage of the world's history, for the exchange of ideals between peoples, and especially between East and West. He was, too, much more than a preacher. While glorifying the Indian past and the ancient contribution of his people to the intellectual wealth of the world, he was a man of modern outlook, incessantly framing concrete schemes for the social regeneration of India. He was bent upon the firm establishment of the Order of Ramakrishna, of which he was the head—an order which he designed not for contemplation alone, but for social service; he would, if he could, have commanded vast resources for educational enterprise; and he was resolved to initiate some definite agency for the education of Indian women. This last was the part of his programme which, from an early stage of their acquaintance, Swami Vivekananda seems to have marked out as the special work of Margaret Noble; and before he left England, at the end of 1896, she had come to recognise the call. A year later she sailed for India, landed at Calcutta in the beginning of 1898, and made her home with some American friends at Belur, on the river a short distance from the city, where was established the headquarters of the Ramakrishna Mission. Soon after her arrival in Bengal she was admitted to the Order by the name of Nivedita (the Dedicated) —thereafter the name by which she was known, far beyond the bounds of her personal activity.

From May to October of her first year in India the Swami, Sister Nivedita, and three other Western women travelled together in the North-West, in Kumaon and Kashmir. The tour, which included a pilgrimage to the famous shrine of Amarnath, was rich in experience, afterwards recorded in *The Master as I Saw Him.* It gave her, as she said in that book, glimpses of "a great religious life of the ancient order, living itself out amidst the full and torturing consciousness of all the anomalies and perplexities of the modern transition." These fruitful journeyings ended in the autumn of 1898, and then it was that Sister Nivedita endeavoured to carry out her project for an Indian school in the Hindu quarter of Calcutta. For reasons which everyone who knows a little of the world of orthodox Hinduism will appreciate, the experiment was attended with much difficulty, and in the course of a few months it was abandoned in order that new means and opportunities might be found. In June 1899, accompanied by Vivekananda, Sister Nivedita left Calcutta for Europe, and during the autumn they were fellow-guests in the house of some invaluable American friends on the Hudson River. The Swami returned to India at the close of 1900. This period of a year and a half furnished Sister Nivedita with most of the opportunities of companionship and discussion which gave her the special point of view which for the rest of her life marked her interpretation of Indian life and thought. She remained in England until the beginning of 1902, when she resumed her work in Calcutta under conditions much more favourable to success than those which had accompanied its beginning. But the personal association from which it had sprung was then almost at an end. Swami Vivekananda died at Belur on July 4, 1902. A few months afterwards Sister Nivedita was joined by an American colleague, Miss Christine Greenstidel, and together they entered upon the work of enlarging the scope of the school in Bose Para Lane, Bagh Bazar. In the early part of the year 1905 a dangerous illness befel Sister Nivedita, and this was followed, in the autumn of 1906, by a long spell of malarial fever, the result of the visit of inquiry and service, described in this volume, which she paid during the rainy season of that year to Eastern Bengal, where the people were suffering miserably from famine and flood. The terrible strain of these two illnesses broke down her magnificent constitution, and physically she was never the same again. The last three years of her life were largely spent in England and America. She returned finally to India in the spring of 1911, and was staying for the customary autumn holiday at Darjeeling when, on October 13, she died—a fortnight before the close of her forty-fourth year. Indian friends only, and those the most devoted, were with her at the last; and the body was given to the fire with the Hindu rites of which she had so often spoken and written.

When people asked, as they constantly did, what Sister Nivedita was doing in India, her own answer was always simple. She was a teacher, and in India she was doing nothing else than applying the principles which she had learned from her own instructors in Europe. The Swami Vivekananda's practical aims had been predominantly educational, and his English disciple went to India primarily under the belief that her own part in the far-reaching work to which he had set his hand was to make a school, in an Indian home, where the methods and ideals of the modern educationist might be brought within the cloistral domain of the Eastern wife and mother. Beginning as a tiny kindergarten, the school grew steadily until it had a large attendance of little Hindu girls up to the marriageable age, and a still larger number of married women and widows. As conducted by Sister Nivedita and her colleague, the school involved no uprooting from familiar surroundings. Neither child nor woman was taken from her home into a foreign world; her schooling demanded only a daily migration from one home to another in the same lane or ward. The principle was, as Sister Nivedita herself expressed it, by means of familiar factors of her daily life so to educate the Indian girl as to enable her to realise those ends which are themselves integral aspirations of that life. There was no attempt to convert her to any religious or social system alien from her own; but rather, by means of her own customs and traditions, to develop her in harmony with Indian ideals, the teachers themselves following those ideals as far as they could be made practicable. It appeared to some that Sister Nivedita, alike in her school and in the zenana, was in certain respects a reactionary influence—upholding the *purdah* and child marriage and perpetual widowhood as institutions essential to the preservation of the society which she had learned to admire. But she was far indeed from seeking to maintain the old unchanged. "Under the old scheme," she said, "women found not only a discipline but a career"; yet she saw that this old scheme was a preparation and an opportunity fitted only to the soil in which it grew. To the Indian as to the European woman the modern revolution has brought a narrowing of her lot, and has wrought havoc with the traditional skill in handicraft. "To-day every Indian woman can cook, and that well. But she cannot sew, and she has nothing but gossip and prayer, when the afternoon siesta is over, wherewith to occupy her leisure." Hence Sister Nivedita and her colleague found it necessary to teach the wives and widows needlework of various kinds. But it may well be that they themselves learned more of the irresistible movement of the modern spirit

b

in the orthodox world of Hinduism, when they found themselves met by an insistent demand from the young wives to be taught English so that they might become in some real sense the companions of their husbands.

The success that attended the Vivekananda school in Bagh Bazar was not of the resounding kind; but it was a most noteworthy sign of the times; and in the later years of Sister Nivedita's life it was prevented only by the narrow means possessed by the Sisters from developing into a great institution. Its influence, however, could never have been measured by the number of its pupils or the amount of regular teaching done within the modest rooms and courts which are described in the opening chapters of this book. How long it took Sister Nivedita to conquer the suspicions of the quiet, proud, and intensely self-respecting people of Bagh Bazar I have no means of knowing: I can speak only of what I saw when, some two or three years after she had made her home among them, I had opportunities of observing her among the surroundings into which she fitted so perfectly. She was then entirely accepted by her Hindu neighbours. All their doors were open to her. In the bazaars and lanes and by the riverside everybody knew her, and she would be saluted as she passed with an affectionate reverence which was beautiful and touching to see. The House of the Sisters was known of all; not as a school merely, but as a centre of unfailing friendliness and succour. The people remembered how, when the plague broke out among them, Sister Nivedita had joined with the brethren of the Order of Ramakrishna in a crusade of nursing and sanative cleansing. And in times when there was no spectacular call of pestilence or flood, there went out from her house a constant stream of social and personal service. For this, as Sister Nivedita always maintained, there was an ever-increasing call under the economic pressure upon the class which, with its more or less of English education, was rendering clerical and professional service to the ruling power.

Beginning thus, with the conviction that the European can work fruitfully in India only upon the basis of perfect co-operation with the children of the soil, Sister Nivedita was led to make the great renunciation. The land to whose service she had devoted herself made an overwhelming appeal to her—its history and thought, its people and their life, its present state in subjection and social transition. There could be no partial surrender with her: she gave herself utterly. Accepting the lot of the Indian woman, living as her neighbours lived, in a little native house severely devoid of all inessentials, she worked among them in all seasons—when the splendid cold weather of Bengal gave place to the terrific heat, and this in turn to the rains which every year made the narrow streets of the quarter into rivulets. "Never have I known such complete self-effacement," wrote her closest Indian woman friend:

> "All the rare gifts that opened out a great career for her in the West she laid at the service of our motherland. . . . She had so completely identified herself with us that I never heard her use phrases like 'Indian need' or 'Indian women': it was always 'our need,' 'our women.' She was never as an outsider who came to help, but one of us who was striving and groping about to find salvation." [1]

It needs not to be said that this was the secret of her extraordinary power. India instinctively understands every form of renunciation, and it would, I conceive, be impossible to exaggerate the impression made by this life of absolute sincerity and self-dedication, with its rejoicing acceptance of the austerity and simplicity of the old Indian order. But this, of course, was not all. No one who knows the India of the past decade will need to be told that the influence of her ideal and example went out from the little house in Bagh Bazar in ever-widening circles as the

[1] Mrs. J. C. Bose, in the *Modern Review* (Calcutta), November 1911.

years went on. Sister Nivedita was the most fervent and convinced of Nationalists: the word continually on her lips was Nationality. She had unbounded faith in the reserve power of the Indian people, and her call to the younger generation was a ringing challenge to them to rise, not only to the height of the past, but to the demand of the future. Unsparing she could be, at times, in criticising the Indian character; but she never bated a jot of her belief in the certainty of its triumph, and it went hard with anyone, European or Asiatic, who offered any kind of insult or disparagement to the people of her adoption. The beginning of her work in India coincided with a stage of extraordinary deadness in public and intellectual life. But the change was already on the way, and she had the joy of seeing the growth of a new spirit, the rapid formation of new ideals, the dawn, as she believed, of a renascent national life and power. The influences that have gone to the shaping of the New India are still obscure; but this may be said with complete assurance, that among them all there has been no single factor that has surpassed, or equalled, the character and life and words of Margaret Noble.

There were no rules of exclusion in the House of the Sisters, provided only that the privileged male visitor did not intrude during the hours given up to the orthodox Hindu ladies who came for tuition in needlework and English. And to one engaged throughout the week in the merciless daily labour that generally falls upon the Englishman in India, the Sundays in Bose Para Lane were a refreshment and a stimulus the memory of which is never likely to pass away. Breakfast was served with the extreme of simplicity on the little veranda, and the group would not break up until long after the morning sun had become too hot for a comfortable journey back through the blazing streets. Her house was a wonderful rendezvous. Not often did one meet a Western visitor, save at those times when an English or American friend would be making a stay in Calcutta; but nowhere else, so far as my experience went, was there an opportunity of making acquaintance with so many interesting types of the Indian world. There would come members of Council and leaders in the public affairs of Bengal; Indian artists, men of letters, men of science; orators, teachers, journalists, students; frequently a travelled member of the Order of Ramakrishna, occasionally a wandering scholar, not seldom a public man or leader of religion from a far province. The experience was beyond expression delightful, and its influence, you knew, was to be felt along many lines.

There was a time, in the years which followed her return from the first of her long visits to the West, when it seemed likely that Sister Nivedita would develop into a regular and constant speaker. She gave frequent addresses, and not in Calcutta alone. In the autumn of 1902 she made a tour in Western India, where she lectured to large audiences. This was succeeded by a similar tour in the Madras Presidency during the same winter, and when at home she was constantly in request as a speaker at meetings large and small. Latterly, however, she showed a disposition to confine her activities to writing and to direct contact with those who were making towards the New India of which she dreamed. Many of her friends approved this change of plan; but it has always seemed to me that public speech gave her the opportunity most adapted to the delivery of her message. She varied greatly, it is true, on the platform. Always rather at the mercy of a too difficult thesis, given to the use of socio-philosophic terms, and following a too compressed method of exposition, she not infrequently soared beyond the comprehension of her audience. She spoke least successfully when under the strain of an important occasion; most brilliantly when responding to the immediate stimulus of a challenge in debate or of a suggestion or incident arising naturally in the meeting. One thinks of her at her best (and how often she was so!) addressing some crowded gathering in the years before her health was broken and before there came upon her that sense of "the petty done, the undone vast," in which latterly she seemed to abide. And from a score or so of occasions, differing greatly in circumstances, I recall especially two as showing her in most characteristic fashion.

The first was during the rainy season of 1902, when she cut short a Sunday evening call at Bagh Bazar by saying that she was due at a lecture. She allowed me to accompany her, and we went to a Bengali school in the university quarter. The quadrangle was densely crowded with youths and men, and on a dais was seated, alongside the symbolic *tulsi* plant, a *Kathak* (one of the last survivals of the ancient minstrels), who as we entered began a recital from the Ramayana. For an hour or so he continued, declaming and intoning, while his hearers listened enrapt and a friendly interpreter explained to me, the one outsider present, the movement of the story. When the recital was finished Sister Nivedita rose to speak, without any preliminary (she always disliked the intrusion of a chairman). She spoke, as always, from the feeling of the moment as regards the expression, from long reflection and conviction as regards the substance. And she began with a reference to the recital to which they had just been listening, pointing her moral swiftly and powerfully. Did they, she asked, think it was enough to learn and admire the ancient stories and to glory in the ideals which had inspired the men and women of early India? "Believe me, that is nothing. The Ramayana is not something that came once for all, from a society that is dead and gone; it is something springing ever from the living heart of a people. Our word to the young Indian to-day is: Make your own Ramayana, not in written stories, but in service and achievement for the motherland."

The other occasion, a year or two later, was one in which, at the first glance, she seemed ex-extraordinarily "out of the picture." The hall of the Dalhousie Institute, Calcutta, was filled with a mixed audience, mostly Indian, for as odd a purpose as could well be imagined in that country—to hear a debate on Marriage *versus* Celibacy. The discussion had been arranged, as an anniversary treat, by the committee of a Bengali public library, and the last of the Military Members of the Viceroy's Council (Sir Edmond Elles) was in the chair. The case for celibacy was stated by the late Sir Edward Law, the Finance Minister; the case for marriage by an elderly Parsee member of the Indian Civil Service. Both openers gave play to the easy facetiousness which is commonly deemed appropriate to the public discussion of this and kindred subjects, and the meeting had reached a low ebb when, towards the end, Sir Edmond Elles called upon Sister Nivedita, who was seated on the platform with an English woman friend. She began slowly, with a courteous half-humorous rebuke to the chairman, and then in a few pointed and searching sentences outlined the conception of wifehood as revealed in Eastern tradition. Developing this, and incidentally crushing some criticism by a previous speaker of the Western woman who makes a career for herself outside marriage, she gave a brilliant little exposition of the contrasted and complementary views of the place of woman as mother and as individual. It was marvellously skilful, complete, and convincing, and the whole thing occupied a bare ten minutes. But what interested one even more than the perfection of the speech was the way in which the tone of the meeting was transformed by the touchstone of her dominating spirit. Many times, before and after that, I heard her speak: to groups of students, or in the Calcutta Town Hall before a great audience, on her one absorbing theme—the religion of Nationalism; to English gatherings in hall or church or drawing-room. And I have thought, and still think, that her gift of speech was something which, when fully exercised, I have never known surpassed—so fine and sure was it in form, so deeply impassioned, of such flashing and undaunted sincerity.

It cannot, perhaps, be said that any of her books fully represent the strength and range of her mind, notwithstanding the fine literary faculty which was undoubtedly hers. As with her speaking so with her writing: it was most effective when it came out in attack or controversy. There are things buried in Indian newspapers and magazines which revealed an extraordinary power of direct and resonant expression, and a grip of argument and affairs which she would not have blamed one for praising as masculine. And yet her books, though so much less wonderful than herself, are surely destined for a larger public than they have yet reached. *Kali the Mother*, the little volume in which she gave the firstfruits of her Indian studies under Vivekananda, showed something of her interpretative faculty, although its title and sentiment were startling to those English readers who knew only the ordinary European view of the "bloody goddess." Into *The Web of Indian Life* she put, as her friends knew, all the force of her mind and all the intensity of her faith. The result was moving and powerful, if unequal: it gave an earnest of what the world might have expected from her had she lived to write the interpretation of Indian domestic life and the social structure of Hinduism to which undoubtedly she would have devoted herself. Her later books display a steady advance in mastery of expression. In *Cradle Tales of Hinduism* she retold a number of the heroic stories of which she made constant use in her lessons and addresses; and in *The Master as I Saw Him*, the last to be published in her lifetime, she gave a picture of the Swami Vivekananda as she had come to know him during the seven years of their association. The task of writing the Life of the teacher to whom she owed the purpose and direction of her own activity, she left to other hands.

No effort has been made in the foregoing rough sketch to portray the personality, the rare and splendid and dauntless spirit, that was Margaret Noble. To do this would be to attempt the impossible. So much of the reality as can be conveyed to those who did not know her will be contained in a collection of Letters and Memorials, which, it is hoped, may before long be brought together. And in the meantime I am enabled to quote a few brief tributes from some who, in England or India, were associated in one way or another with her work and her ideal.

Nothing that she touched remained commonplace; her letters, much more than her books, disclose the temper and genius that were known to her friends and fellow-workers. Her dominant notes were clarity and sincerity and an incomparable vitality. She was, of all the men and women one has known, the most vividly alive. Having renounced all that most of us hold dearest, she had the right to be earnest and to demand earnestness; but not in the smallest degree did the overmastering purpose of her being remove her from the sphere of personal relations. At all times she toiled with an absolute concentration; her inner life was intense, austere, and deeply controlled. Yet never was anyone more wholly and exquisitely human, more lovely and spontaneous in the sharing of daily services and joys. Professor Geddes has recalled the infinite changefulness of her moods. They ran, in truth, over the whole scale: from the fierceness and scorn of which Mr. Nevinson speaks to a sparkling playfulness that made her, in India as in the West, the life and light of her circle. In matters of personal conduct, as in weightier affairs of public or social activity, she was an unequalled counsellor: so extraordinary in its rapidity and sureness was her judgment. And those to whom she gave the ennobling gift of her friendship knew her as the most perfect of comrades, while they hold the memory of that gift as this world's highest benediction. They think of her years of sustained and intense endeavour, of her open-eyed and impassioned search for truth, of the courage that never quailed, the noble compassionate heart; they think of her tending the victims of famine and plague, or ministering day by day among the humble folk with whom her lot was cast: putting heart into the helpless and defeated, showing to the young and perplexed the star of a glowing faith and purpose, royally spending all the powers of a rich intelligence and an overflowing humanity for all who called upon her in their need. And some among them count it an honour beyond all price that they were permitted to share, in however imperfect a measure, the mind and confidence of this radiant child of God.

S. K. RATCLIFFE.

21 BUCKINGHAM STREET, LONDON, W.C.,
July 1913.

A FEW TRIBUTES

Professor Patrick Geddes

Our acquaintance began in New York early in 1900, and continued into intimacy and collaboration during the following summer, at that meeting of the International Association which became the Summer School of the Paris Exhibition of that in many ways memorable year. Actively occupied as a guide to many of its departments, and carrying on a peripatetic interpretation of them upon lines of regional and occupational evolution, broadly akin to those of Le Play and his disciples, I found no one who so rapidly and ardently seized upon the principle and delighted in every application of it as Sister Nivedita.

Eager to master these evolutionary methods, and to apply them to her own studies, to Indian problems therefore above all, she settled above our home into an attic cell, which suited at once her love of wide and lofty outlooks and her ascetic care of material simplicity ; and there she worked, for strenuous weeks. She has generously recognised, at the opening of *The Web of Indian Life,* how thus coming "to understand a little of Europe," she had been given indirectly a method by which to interpret her Indian experiences—while for my part I must no less recognise how her keener vision and more sympathetic and spiritual insight carried her discernment of the rich and varied embroidery of the Indian web far beyond that simple texture of the underlying canvas, of the material conditions of life, which it was my privilege at the outset of our many conversations to help her to lay hold upon.

The whole personality of Nivedita—her face, her voice, her changing moods and daily life, were ever expressing the alternating reaction of outward environment and inward spirit which goes on throughout the individual and social life. She was open at once to the concrete and the abstract, to the scientific and the philosophic, and her many moods were in perpetual interplay—sparkling with keen observation, with humorous or poetic interpretation, or, opal-like, suffused with mystic light, aflame with moral fire. All came out in her talks, her occasional lectures—each a striking improvisation—now in gentlest persuasiveness leading her audience into sympathetic understanding, or even approval, of some aspect or feature of Indian life, unknown or perhaps repellent before; or again, bursting into indignant flash and veritable thunder upon our complacent and supercilious British philistinism.

With children she was at once a born teacher and a skilled. She would sit with them upon the floor in the firelight and tell them her *Cradle Tales of Hinduism*, with a power and charm even excelling her written version of them, so touching this or that ardent young soul to dream of following her to the utmost East. Or she might give them a literature lesson—say, on Shelley's Skylark—and here demand, and arouse, their observation and their imagination in touch with the poet's. This union of sense and symbol, which we too easily let slip apart, was ever with her. Thus of our many memory portraits, none comes back more vividly than of her in autumn twilight, now crooning, now chanting, the *Hymn to Agni* over the glowing, dying embers of a garden-fire. Strange though the words were, we still hear the refrain. It was the tongue, the music, of Orient in Occident, the expression of spirit in nature—a face, a voice, aglow with energy, at peace with night. P. GEDDES.

MR. NEVINSON

It is as vain to describe Sister Nivedita in two pages as to reduce fire to a formula and call it knowledge. There was, indeed, something flame-like about her, and not only her language but her whole vital personality often reminded me of fire. Like fire, and like Shiva, Kali, and other Indian powers of the spirit, she was at once destructive and creative, terrible and beneficent. There was no dull tolerance about her, and I suppose no one ever called her gentle. Even with friends her disagreement could be vehement, and her contradiction was very direct. In face of the enemy her eyes turned to glowing steel, and under anger they deepened in colour, like Garibaldi's. Her scorn of presumptuous ignorance and her indignation at wrong were blasting. I do not doubt that rage lacerated her own heart, but she withered the enemy up. No one would call her gentle.

But of all nobly sympathetic natures she was among the finest. She identified herself with the Indians among whom she lived as barely half a dozen men or women from these islands have done before. I do not mean merely by her adoption of Hindu symbolism for thought, nor by her purified form of Hindu worship. To me, thought and religion are so much the outcome of physical nature, of nationality, and ancient association or descent, that it seems hardly possible for a foreigner, born outside those overwhelming influences, to make another people's thought and religion genuinely his own. Explicable, and even reasonable, as her worship in the temple beside the Ganges was, it seemed a little strained and exotic for one of our race—a little self-conscious and unreal, like an Englishman going about in the beautiful Indian dress. But her readiness to accept and interpret what was clearest and highest in Hindu thought, her capacity not merely for understanding Indian life, but for discovering and so intensifying the ideal in its customs, and the indignant revolt kindled in her by the insolence, degradation, and maiming restriction to which every subject race is necessarily exposed—from such imaginative sympathy, I think, arose the extraordinary power which she exercised over the more thoughtful and active of the Indian patriots around her. I do not know whether on the religious side it could be said of her, as of the philosopher, that she was "drunk with God"; but on the side of daily life and political thought it might certainly be said that she was drunk with India.

Her greatest book, *The Web of Indian Life*, reveals the ideal of the Indian spirit with great beauty, and in it there is a passage which seems to illustrate the contrast between the ordinary Anglo-Indian woman's aspect of India and her own. She is saying how differently Niagara would have been regarded if it had been situated on the Ganges:

> Instead of fashionable picnics and railway pleasure-trips, the yearly or monthly incursion of worshipping crowds. Instead of hotels, temples. Instead of ostentatious excess, austerity. Instead of the desire to harness its mighty forces to the chariot of human utility, the unrestrainable longing to throw away the body, and realise at once the ecstatic madness of Supreme Union.

Spiritual as she was, here was no impracticable or dreamy spirit. Whether teaching in her little school among poor Indian streets of Calcutta, or struggling against the famine and exploitation of Eastern Bengal, or awakening in young India the spirit which marked the growing consciousness of nationality, her eye was fixed not only on some eternal absorption in the infinite, but on the eternal issues of the present moment here. We might say of her as has been said of the *Gita:*

> The book is really a battle-cry. Spirituality is with it no retreat from men and things, but a burning fire of knowledge that destroys bondage, consumes sluggishness and egoism, and penetrates everywhere. Not the withdrawn, but the transfigured life, radiant with power and energy, triumphant in its selflessness, is religion.

Sister Nivedita always appeared to me to act on the *Gita's* own stirring exhortation, "Holding gain and loss as one, prepare for battle." She herself was thus always prepared. For a spirit like hers was not likely to meet with anything but battle in this world, and it is as a soldier in the War of Liberation that I remember her—a soldier with a flaming sword. H. W. NEVINSON.

PROFESSOR CHEYNE, D.D., D.LITT., F.B.A.

The beautiful character of Sister Nivedita is well known to her friends, but needs to be brought before outsiders, especially those of the younger generation. She was like a star, if we should not rather say, like a sun, and it would be sad if this sun should altogether set. Her place can hardly be filled in the present æon, though one or another may arise who may remind the well-equipped historical student of her. Once in the last century, however, Vivekananda and his disciple Nivedita have had their prototypes: I refer to the saintly and heroic religious and social reformers known respectively as the Bab and Kurratu'l-'Ayn ("Refreshment of the eyes"). The latter illustrious pair lived and worked primarily for Persia, the former for India, but both had a sense that their principles could only have adequate recognition when all nations accepted them as their standard of right. The Bab and "Her Highness the Pure" were, however, much less modern than Vivekananda and Nivedita: it is Baha 'Ullah, and especially his son and successor Abdul Baha, who first in modern times have consciously undertaken in a practical manner to blend the characteristic qualities of East and West.

It is the modernity of these Indian reformers which attracts. But then it must be remembered that they come at the end of a long period which goes back as far as Rammohun Roy. Nivedita, though "dedicated" to the service of India, and so far as was possible Hinduised, never ceased to keep in touch with Western thinkers and reformers: her visits to her earlier fatherland sufficiently prevented this. The intellectual department in which she was really a stranger was the critical study of the Christian Scriptures; it was the reading of a small book of mine called *Bible Problems*, and perhaps, I may add, the example of a critic who was also a preacher of the Gospel, which I set, which revealed to her the possibilities she had missed. And yet I do not question that all is for the best. It was better that Nivedita and I should work independently from different points of view, and in order that a larger point of view might emerge in the future. She was well aware that her teacher had not himself reached the goal, and that West and East would have to join hands to pass the difficult region on the other side of which dwells Religious Truth. And I too am fully conscious of the deficiencies of my own stock of knowledge. It is to Sister Nivedita I owe it that these deficiencies are not greater than they are.

At this point I venture to quote what I have said elsewhere (in the *Modern Review*, Calcutta, February 1912):

"It was *The Web of Indian Life* which brought us spiritually together. The book fascinated me. I had never before seen India described from the inside. I wrote to her as warmly as I felt, at the same time drawing her attention to the criticisms which some dryasdust professor had brought against her views of history. She replied in glowing terms, at the same time answering my inquiry as to the best sources of information for Hindu religion in its noblest form. She pointed me to the *Bhagavad Gita* and the lectures of the Swami Vivekananda. This produced a revolution in my view of the capacity of Hindu religion for adapting itself progressively to the spiritual needs of Indians, and for contributing elements of enormous value to the purification, enrichment, and reinterpretation of Christianity. . . . Sister Nivedita was well aware that I looked for help to the Aryan East, and especially to her and her Master, and this may have been the chief reason why she paid me in the dazzling coin of affection, reverence, and gratitude for the sympathy which I delighted to express to her."

T. K. CHEYNE.

MR. RABINDRANATH TAGORE

[The following passages are translated from an appreciation of Sister Nivedita contributed by Mr. Rabindranath Tagore, the poet of Bengal, to a vernacular magazine soon after her death.]

She had a versatile, all-round genius, and with that there was another thing in her nature: that was her militancy. She had power, and she exerted that power with full force on the lives of others. A great enthusiasm to take possession of the mind after conquering it worked in her nature. . . . I have not noticed in any other human being the wonderful power that was hers of absolute dedication of herself. In her own personality there was nothing which could stand in the way of this utter self-dedication. No bodily need, weakness, or craving; no European habit which had grown up from infancy; no family affection or tender tie of kinship; no slight received from her own people; no indifference, weakness, and want of self-sacrifice on the part of those for whom she had devoted her life, could turn her aside. He who has seen her has seen the essential form of man, the form of the spirit. It is a piece of great good fortune to be able to see how the inner being of man reveals itself with unobstructed and undiminished energy and effulgence, nullifying the obstruction of all outer material coatings or impediments. We have been blessed in that we have witnessed that unconquered nobility of man in Sister Nivedita. . . . The life which Sister Nivedita gave for us was a very great life. There was no defrauding of us on her part—that is, she gave herself up fully for the service of India; she did not keep anything back for her own use. Every moment of every day she gave whatever was best in her, whatever was noblest. For this she underwent all the privation and austerity that is possible for man. Her resolve was this and this alone—that she would give only that which was absolutely genuine; she would not mix self with it in the least;—no, not her hunger or thirst, profit or loss, name or fame; neither fear nor shrinking, nor ease nor rest. . . . She was in fact a Mother of the People. We had not seen before an embodiment of the spirit of motherhood which, passing beyond the limits of the family, can spread itself over the whole country. We have had some idea of the sense of duty of man in this respect, but had not witnessed the whole-hearted mother-love of women. When she uttered the words "Our People," the tone of absolute kinship which struck the ear was not heard from any other among us. Whoever has seen what reality there was in her love of the people, has surely understood that we—while giving perhaps our time, our money, even our life—have not been able to give them our heart; we have not acquired the power to know the people as absolutely real and near. . . . The man who does not see the people, the nation, in every man, may say with his lips what he likes, but he does not see the country properly. I have seen that Sister Nivedita *saw* the common people, *touched* them, did not simply think of them mentally. The respect with which she would greet some ordinary Mussulman woman dwelling in a hut in a village is not possible for an ordinary individual; for the vision that enables one to see the greatness of humanity in humble individuals is a very uncommon gift. It was because this vision was so natural to her that she did not lose her respect for India in spite of the nearness of her life to the life of the people of India for so long a time.

BOOKS BY SISTER NIVEDITA

Kali the Mother. 1900. Swan Sonnenschein & Co.
The Web of Indian Life. 1904. W. Heinemann.
Cradle Tales of Hinduism. 1907. Longmans.
An Indian Book of Love and Death. 1908. Longmans.
The Master as I Saw Him: Being Pages from the Life of the Swami Vivekananda. London: Longmans; Calcutta: *Ubodhan* Office, Bagh Bazar.
Civic and National Ideals. 1911. Calcutta: *Ubodhan* Office.
Studies from an Eastern Home. 1913. Longmans.

In preparation:

Myths of the Indo-Aryan Race (Stories from the Mahabharata).
Footfalls of Indian History.
Essays on Indian Education.
Religion and Dharma.

The greater part of the chapters composing this volume appeared first as contributions to Indian newspapers and magazines. Acknowledgments are made in especial to the Editors of the *Modern Review* and the *Statesman* (Calcutta).

STUDIES FROM AN EASTERN HOME

LIFE IN THE HINDU QUARTER OF CALCUTTA

When I first discovered that my work would mean living in the Hindu quarter of Calcutta, the usual protests were forthcoming on all sides. One would have supposed that the chances of immediate death from cholera or typhoid were to chances of safety as fifty to one. I have not seen this alarm justified, however. I have been here now for some months without finding any reason for a day's illness.

My home is, in my eyes, charming. With its two courtyards, its limited second story, and its quaintly-terraced roofs, built at five different levels, it is a rambling specimen of the true old Hindu style of building. In the whole place there is not an inch of glass; the lower casements are protected by iron, and the upper by wooden bars, and so, while the sunlight outside my little study is softened by mats made of dark green splints, my bedroom is always open to the stars. Here some large family has lived in days gone by, and here maybe at least one generation has died off, and then, when the last of the older members was gone, those remaining would break up into smaller groups, again to become the nuclei of fresh communities. Crowded with memories the old house seems, of such lives as are passing continually beneath my windows, in the lane and the villages without—ignorant and unsophisticated doubtless, but full of human tenderness and simple worship.

The lane is quite clean and so charmingly irregular. First on one side and then on the other it gives a twist, and wherever there is a space between the larger houses little villages have grown up. Here is one, a cluster of mud huts, with their rich brown walls and their red-tiled roofs, nestling at the foot of a cluster of cocoanut palms. High up against the blue these wave their plumes, and below their long shadows lie across a tiny tank and the roof of the cowhouse and protect a few green things under the wall. To another village the pump-like hydrant is the entrance, almost always surrounded by its veiled women, carrying their beautiful waterpots of brass or earthenware. Everywhere the happy laughter of children in the sunlight, everywhere the flutter of newly-washed drapery hung out to dry, every here and there a cow or two.

Here, at my writing-table, surrounded by the books and pictures and the simple refinements of modern life, I look out on a world of many centuries ago. Nay, it is with me here within my doors. I can never forget the day when my old waiting-woman came to consult me about the purchase of a cooking-stove—to cost six farthings. Armed with this mighty sum she purchased three small iron bars, a large thin tile, and a little heap of Ganges mud, out of which she proceeded to construct a modest hearthplace of her own. On top of this she used, for cooking, a round earthen pot with a groove in the neck, and some days later she very diffidently requested another six farthings to buy something like a pair of tongs with which to clasp this when hot. It was a slight and curious-looking utensil, and I suppose no man could say how long her ancestors have regarded its exact fellows as harmless luxuries of housekeeping. The whole thing was eloquent of poverty, bravely met and decently borne through many generations. Still more significant was it, however, to hear her crying gently when she found her earthen pot, not unnaturally, cracked over the fire. Its value was just one farthing! This old woman is over seventy, and I, less than half her age, call her "Jhee" or "daughter." Even tiny children of higher rank call her, however, by this name, according to the beautiful custom of Hindu households, where to the women-servants the master and mistress are "father" and "mother," and the daughters "jewel sisters." Nothing is commoner than for these old attendants to attach themselves to a family as grandmother, claiming the privilege of scolding their employers and spoiling those employers' children to the end of their days. In such cases the social inferiority of this member of the family group would not be easily perceived by a stranger. The mistress prepares her servant's food and gives it with her own hand (a curious inversion of our notions), and when the servant dies, in the fulness of time, she is mourned by these kindred of her adoption as one of their own blood.

The number of services that Jhee could not perform made my early days interesting. On my second afternoon, when I turned to her for hot water for my tea-tray, I was amused to see her suddenly disappear. It was only for a moment, and she came back dripping, having found it necessary to take a bath before touching what I was about to eat. Exaggerations of this sort gradually disappeared of their own accord, and now, strange to say, she condescends to wash my cups and saucers, though when another *mem-sahib* visits me I find I must do this for my friend myself. These Indian superstitions about food would surely repay elaborate study. But why has the notion of purification always been overladen with so many inconveniences and restrictions in Asiatic countries, while in old Greece it was apparently passed over with such lightness and grace?

My house has a courtyard. Why do we English carry the domestic architecture that is appropriate to the British Isles into this Eastern land of sun and shine? Would it not be wise to take up the style of the country? The Hindu certainly contrives to keep himself cooler than we do, and the great marble courts that we see in rich men's houses, with plants grouped against their steps and pillars, must be as beautiful as anything in Athens or Pompeii. Mine is no floor of pure white marble, yet it was long before I discovered the secret of the pleasure that I took in opening my front door on my return in the evening. Then I found that it was the meeting again with the sky and stars within. A great well of coolness and shadow in the daytime, and a temple of eternity at night, a playground of merry breezes, and an open sundial—who would not love a house with a courtyard?

The other architectural beauty of my home is its roof. Up there one pictures oneself in Syria. Away in all directions stretch similar housetops, broken by the green of trees and gardens, and diversified by colonnades, and balustrades, and steep stone staircases. The rich crowded beauty of Lahore is not here on the great flats of Bengal. The impression is rather of breadth and solitude, roofs and palm tufts, and the vast dome above. Here, at dawn or sunset or in the moonlight, one can feel alone with the whole universe. Down below, with the smoke rising from little fires of cooking as the evening meal is cooked within each court, how different from the cosy rural scene one would see in England! But then how different, too, above! And this although in both it is that glimpse of fire that makes the glow of home-coming. For we must not forget the radiant purity of this upper air and the large luminousness of moon and stars.

To the Hindu woman, cooped up for the most part in her zenana, how much it means to possess such a roof. Here is her whole outlook on life—life in the abstract, life on the impersonal scale. Here is the neighbourhood of other women, for the roof of one zenana is often accessible to another; here are coolness and merry talk in the long hours of summer nights, when all the girls of the family steal away to sleep where it is also possible to breathe; and here also is that glimpse of the Ganges that is the lightener of toil and bringer of refreshment as of worship. Beautiful

Ganges! How she is loved of her children, and how quaintly delicate is that salutation to the river when, ere stepping into her and so soiling her with their feet, they stoop and place a little of the water on their heads.

"But hark, hark! the dogs do bark! The beggars are coming to town." A very practical question to the Indian house-mother is that of beggars. In a perfect troop they come down the lane, though fortunately not every day: numbers of well-dressed, good-humoured-looking men and women, clad in white for the most part, with large rosaries, tramping along, staff in one hand and begging-bowl in the other. Such complete social recognition do they receive that the city is actually mapped out in wards for their peregrinations, according to the day of the week. It is the solitary mendicant, however, who interests me most. Theoretically, in the great majority of cases, he is a barefooted friar, so to speak, wearing the yellow robes that Buddha wore and appealing for alms in the strength of the Sacred Name. Perhaps he was already within the doors when one heard it first, and there he stands repeating the sonorous *Haribol!* or the *Sita Ram!* which constitutes a prayer. This Indian feeling about the Name of God is very striking. To repeat it is the whole of supplication, and they argue that, if putting the hand into a fire burns, whether we feel it or not, shall not the cry to the Almighty do good whether we know it or not? But maybe our friend remains still to sing a song, and this is worth marking, for a whole literary form of great sweetness and power is devoted to the service of these beggars; and not many years ago all that now remains of the exquisite ballad-songs of Ram Prasad, the Robert Burns of Bengal, had to be collected from just such sources as this. The author is always supposed to include his own name in the last couplet, and it will be seen at once how useful this quaint canon would prove to the collector of the works of a particular song-maker. Very little, a tiny pinch of rice or a few fruits or the smallest of coin, will content our friend, but more could hardly be given when the claims are so many. There is no stigma in the mind of the giver, however, attaching to the man who had to say, "Mother, give me food." The dictum that the "starving man has a natural right to his neighbour's bread" would rouse no responsive thrill in India, where something very like it is taken as a fundamental social axiom.

Full of unlooked-for interests is the life here—amongst "new men, strange faces, other minds." A few inches off my table as I write are the constant flutter of wings and the sounds of the voices of birds; yet a little further the waving of trees—the *neem*, and the bo-tree, and the palms—

and underneath and all about a life throbbing with newness yet aglow with the secrets of the past. I look at my Whitman and Wordsworth and the exquisite beauty of the "Beata Beatrix," and I long to be able to pass from the one psychic atmosphere to the other at will, a transition without which the mere accident of physical presence is worth little. Yet as I utter the wish it is already to some small extent answered, and I have perceived a larger existence than I had conceived before—a certain immense life of Humanity, in which time and distance are alike merged, and where the Eastern and the Western Aryan have become one in their noblest manifestations, as Walt Whitman saw it:—

> "Sail, sail thy best ship, O Democracy,
> Of value is thy freight, 'tis not the Present only,
> The Past is also stored in thee;
> Thou holdest not the venture of thyself alone, not of the Western Continent alone,
> Earth's résumé entire floats on thy keel, O ship, is steadied by thy spars,
> With thee time voyages in trust, the antecedent nations sink or swim with thee,
> With all their ancient struggles, martyrs, heroes, epics, wars, thou bear'st the other continents,
> Theirs, theirs as much as thine, the destination port triumphant.
> Steer then with good strong hand and wary eye, O helmsman! Thou carriest great companions,
> Venerable, priestly Asia sails this day with thee,
> And royal Feudal Europe sails with thee."

OUR ZENANA TERRACE

THOSE learned and artistic persons who now and then find their way to us in the midst of the Hindu quarter here in Calcutta, to spend an hour or two, will sometimes break off from their preoccupation with mediæval art and modern monstrosity to assure us that the lane outside our door is a genuine bit of Early Italian loveliness. We like to hear this stated, though we had not needed to be told that our home was beautiful. In the mists of November evenings, when a couple of street lamps, swung from wall brackets at long distances, serve to light up the irregular house-fronts—that stand side by side as if treading on each other's toes in subdued and solemn eagerness—we could not have doubted that our lane was very lovely. Here a small verandah carries the front backwards; there a wall crowds forward, as if to see. The handsome old mouldings round some doorway, again, are half obscured under successive coats of plaster. And everywhere their dress of whitewash gives these substantial Indian buildings a look as of tall persons, decorously wrapped from head to foot in the white and unsewn garments of the East, or, mayhap, at the clear black midnight, thrills one with a suggestion of the pale and sheeted dead.

But if those strangers who have beauty in their hearts can be so affected by our Indian lane, what would they say could they see with our eyes our zenana terrace? Has the reader, in his Western home, some favourite window, with view of lawn and trees, and fringed in early spring with bursting bulbs, or some specially beloved ingle-nook, where fire and picture and low seat make cosy welcome, filling him with the sense of light and peace? In that case he can understand what our terrace is to us. Third of our four courtyards, it opens on the level of the second story. Rooms with higher roofs surround it on three sides, and on the fourth it is enclosed by a high wall, part of which is pierced, to form a screen. In the centre, perfect in its simplicity, a light wooden railing, with four stone corner-posts, protects us from the danger of a fall into the court below. And from the south-east angle of the terrace a narrow staircase, ending in a square and solid tower, climbs steeply up to the roofs and terraces above. Oh, that staircase! By it Crivelli's Angel of Annunciation might fittingly descend, as Herald of God, to seek below her who was blessed amongst all women. Of one thing at least we may be sure ; between Crivelli's Angel and his staircase there would in that case be no disparity.

Or we turn in the opposite direction, and, overtopping the western wall, rise the gnarled boughs and fernlike leafage of a *neem* tree. Planted according to old Calcutta custom beside a neighbour's house, to ward off the malaria that comes with the east winds, this tree of healing is our perpetual joy. Constant breath and motion does it give. In, out, and about it play the sparrows, safe in its hiding from all their foes, while human creatures talk, or gravely sit and watch, below. Nor are the sparrows all its guests. On its outmost branches perch the crows—so full of humour though they cannot laugh! We take but little notice of these aggressive gentlemen, though we are well aware that our mode of life is to them a subject of perpetual curiosity, and they frequently warn and advise us as to the ways of their own kind, with the friendliest intentions. A crow's manner makes one feel that his information of to-day would, if possible, be his instructions of to-morrow. And the pigeons come—the pigeons who live downstairs, in the front courtyard, and sometimes talk the whole night long. Or a single kingfisher will arrive, and for a couple of weeks together will give his loud clear call from the same spot at the same hour, every day, and then fly away. But what we love best are the little birds, and there are many—the tiny *tun-tun*, so much smaller than the sparrow, and an occasional *maina*, and now and then a down-swooping swallow, with other kinds whose names we do not even know. Yes, and as in the early morning or late afternoon we watch the birds that fly in flocks, away and away to the north, with the sunlight shining on their white breasts and under-wings, we know that if to these our dwelling-place offer any landmark we owe it all to the *neem* tree that lives by our side. By its graciousness and beauty alone are won what place we may enjoy in the lives and counsels of the birds.

And something, however little, there surely is. In India all the small birds and beasts that seek the shelter of the house are holy. They come in the train of Lakshmi, the Goddess of Fortune, and show that her presence is about us. And it was a yellow-clad *fakir* who, seated with us one day in silent watching of the loves and quarrels, the faithfulness and mutual forgiveness of the sparrows, suddenly broke his musing with the words, "How wonderful that they can live thus without a scripture!"

But our terrace wall, with the bed of flowers and creeper that runs along it, turns a corner. From west it bends some short way to the north. The way is very short, for here begin the dwelling.

rooms again. But in this end is the perforated curtain-like screen through which the women-folk may take a furtive look at as much of the gay world as can be seen in the neighbouring quarter. And above it, but at some distance beyond, rise, to the sight of a watcher within the house, the tall green-turbaned heads of a line of cocoanut palms. One behind the other they stand, a procession that faces the light as it rises in the east. An hour passes, and it strikes level against the underside of their upright fronds, and then, for ten minutes or so, an anthem, of light thrown back, is chanted to the ascending sun. Then all again grows grey, veiled in the excessive radiance of the tropics, and day wears on. But the morning glory of the palm-trees is not all. The afternoon has come, and at an hour before sunset the eastward-shining beams once more strike level with the great green crowns. This time, however, the sun-rays are caught on the upper surface of low-hanging down-curved leaves, and so twice every day the palm-trees worship God ; and Hindu eyes, trained to seek and respond to the cosmic spectacle, look out from secluded dwellings behind enclosing walls to note this, the matins and evensong of light.

Earlier and later float down to us, on the terrace, the sound of bells rung in the prayer-room of each neighbouring household at the hour of worship. Or again, in the moment of twilight, ere yet the young moon is clear above the *neem*, there come as is fit great thoughts, wide rendings of the veil that hides the Infinite. For this terrace of ours, this hearth of the soul, is silent and hidden and distant from the world, and whether at midnight in the starlight, or seated in the daytime within the shadow of the wall, or even lingering in the sun about the doorways, it is impossible there to forget Crivelli's Angel, or to do aught but await, passive and half-expectant, the inflood of the Divine upon the heart of man.

THE HINDU WIDOW AND THE ZENANA

THE great distinction of Hindu life in English eyes is its vast antiquity. Even its trifles are hoary with age. In the glimpses we catch of the heroic lovers, Sita and Rama, wandering the forest, Sita wears the *sari*, and follows behind her husband, as she might to-day. No one, I suppose, can tell how old the *sari* may be. We see it in Egyptian pictures of the goddesses, and if we remember that it is essentially a strip of cloth, unsewn, we shall find it also, I think, in Greek sculpture.

The notion, current for centuries amongst the orthodox, that to wear anything stitched was utterly unholy, has kept this garment in its primitive simplicity. Like many perfect things, it withholds its complete loveliness at first from even the most enthusiastic eye. It takes months of familiarity to enable the ordinary observer to appreciate to the full the long curves of the veil, the dainty poses of the head, and the exquisite adjustment of every movement to the drapery.

At first, perhaps, we feel that the *sari* is narrow at the ankles, and that the ovoid form, therefore, verges on the "bundle." Then it dawns on us that even this is beautiful, and that there is, moreover, a variety that at first escaped us. It is not drawn so tight, except for some special emergency or effort, and in times of leisure it gives to the feet all the freedom of the skirt. Now and then a breeze catches the veil, and we get—down here in common human life—a moment's glimpse of the Sistine Madonna.

Aubrey Beardsley and Phil May, and the delightful artists of the French poster, have not been wrong in their rapturous interpretation of tennis-blouses and picture-hats and the modiste's fashion-plate. But if we want some soul to gain the vision of the spiritual depths of mere living, to know how one life is tense with agony and another light with the ease of a summer day, to realise for himself the hair's-breadth difference that puts eternal separation between the curves of the Mother of Sorrows and the Mother Crowned, —if we desire this revelation, we may find it in the Hindu zenana. For there we come upon a dignity and grace, with a superb indifference to great or little, that lifts the meanest drudgery, and puts it in the matter of beautiful doing on a level with the harvesting of corn or the facing of death. Only Millet in modern Europe has known this potentiality of common things. He stands alone, for that brooding presence of the Eternal with which *The Angelus* is charged is as different from our nineteenth-century realism as the stories of Nausicaa and Penelope from *A Window in Thrums*. But Millet never came to India, and even if he had come, he alas, would have found himself mere man.

And then the colour of the *sari!* My own experience has been that when a thing was just right I have often failed at first to recognise it. I have had to grow to it. I used to long for *saris* without borders. That little line, meandering up and down the figure, seemed a useless interruption of the composition, a jarring element in the picture; to-day it is like the brush-line of a great master, defining and emphasizing the whole.

But it is not the border only. Whoever knew a Hindu make a mistake in colour? Dark blue is never blue, but purple. Green is like grass lying in sunlight, or shot with rose. Grey is not altogether silver; there is a suggestion of the blue rock-pigeon in it too. A check, or a dazzling combination of black and white, is an outrage impossible to perpetrate.

And yet, and yet, is there anything like the radiant purity of the widow's plain white cloth? Silk for worship, cotton for daily service—but always white, without a touch of colour. Perhaps its charm lies in its associations. The austere simplicity speaks of the highest only. A heart free to embrace the world, a life all consecrated, a past whose sorrow makes the present full of giving—these are the secrets that the widow's *sari* tells.

For it must be understood that this bereavement is regarded in India as a direct call to the religious life. It is the only way in which what is known in Catholic countries as "a vocation" can come to the Hindu woman. Her life henceforth is to be given to God, not to man; and this idea, coupled with an exaggerated respect for celibacy, gives to the widow, and especially to her who has been a child-widow, a unique position of influence in the household. This feeling of reverence persists long after the sentiments of orthodoxy—admiration for long hours spent in worship and for severe asceticism—have disappeared. Hence it was a modern Hindu, of the school calling itself Reformed, who said to me, "The most stately garment in India is the white *sari* of the widow."

Of course all ordeals are hard on some members of the community, and there is little to choose between the injustice of one set of institutions and another. I do not know that the Indian woman of the upper classes, doomed to live from childhood without the closest companionship, is more than conventionally conscious of special hardship. Her vocation is none of her own choosing, but she often throws her whole heart into it for all that, and that wealth of devotion, amounting to absorption, which she would have bestowed upon her husband, goes into the discipline of her own character. And what a character that often is! The most ideal woman I have ever known is the orthodox Brahmin widow. And she does not stand alone. In her I have learned to understand the feeling of the Hindu who, having been received in distinguished society in England, turns from all the elegance and high breeding of European womanhood to find something that surpasses these in that simple unlettered dignity and sweetness of her who was his mother.

The feeling of the Indian family for the little sister who comes home to it a nun is often very tender. Just that grieved acquiescence in a higher consecration than common, which we might show to one dear to ourselves, is theirs. In the past it was no unusual thing for the parents and brothers and sisters, under these circumstances, to take up all her obligations and share them with her. I know one man in whose childhood this went on until the young widow noticed that only vegetable food was being eaten around her, and herself bought fish and cooked it, thus insisting on freeing the others from their self-imposed privation.

The *ekadasi*, or one day of fasting, which falls in every fifteen, is indeed a hardship, and especially so in the hot weather; for not only may no food be taken for twenty-four hours, but not even a drop of water may pass the lips. Yet even this is not a torture invented to make the wretched still more wretched. It was once binding on every good Hindu, and is still retained by astonishingly many. I know one Indian prince who keeps it to the letter; and the most conservative class of all—the high-caste widow, the very type of piety—naturally clings to it more persistently than others. I have never known a man who did not honestly try to mitigate the force of the observance; and I hear that the strictness with which it is kept in Calcutta is unknown elsewhere.

I once met a violent agnostic who was friendly to a single text in the Bible: "He that will be chief among you, let him be your servant." "That," my friend was fond of saying, "comes true every time." But since I have been in India I have seen it in a new light. It reads now like a picture from Oriental domesticity. Here, among women at least, administration is apt to pass directly into service. Of course in large community-houses, with their forty or fifty persons paying allegiance to one head of the family, the mere giving out of stores by the mother-in-law is a serious matter, leaving little time for regular housework. But even this lady, in the course of the day, may pass into the kitchen to cook the food of her husband and herself.

We shall never understand until we realise that passionate self-abnegation is the root of most things. Custom, it is true, petrifies everything till this impulse may sometimes be hardly conscious. But it is often intensely so. I was feasting late one evening with a rich Hindu family, and noticing that even the gentlemen were waiting till I had dined, I made some playful remark to the daughter of the house—whose guest especially I was—about the hardship of *her* part in eating last of all. "Oh," she said, drawing back hurriedly, as if touched on a tender point, "but we like it best so." For this reason, when asked to breakfast, one should never, I think, be late. Whatever the hour of one's arrival and departure, one may be sure that the hostess will not taste food till it is past.

Old prejudices, however, are passing away, and it is now no uncommon thing for a man to begin the day with a cup of tea, while almost all the children of those who can afford it have a sweet-meat and a glass of milk on waking up. But it is rare indeed for the mother to permit herself the luxuries that she dispenses to those around her. And even to this extent many families would refuse to go.

The first duty of the day is the cleaning of one's own room and the zenana department generally. No doubt very rich persons have this done by women servants, but in most houses it is the work of the owner of the room and of her young daughters-in-law. And almost every lady, however rich, does something, either her husband's room or the family chapel, with her own hands. This happens at somewhere near four o'clock. I have never succeeded in rising so early that the rest of the house was still uncleansed.

The next proceeding is that kind of devotion known as meditation. This lasts for at least an hour, and while it is in progress the dawn comes. Then there is the visit to the Ganges for one of the many daily baths, with perhaps the reading of some sacred book till it is time to go. Next, the worship, with all its ritual, that comes nearest to our family prayers, and after all this a meal. It may be necessary to cook this meal with one's own hands before eating. Or beggars may come at the last minute, and then the whole of the food will be given to them, and the lady of the house will go on waiting till her share is once more ready. In this way it is often two o'clock, and I have heard of its being eleven at night, before the head of a large household will breakfast, and this would not count as an austerity.

It is after this meal, about half-past twelve or one o'clock, that the pleasures of life begin for the zenana lady. First, she has a couple of hours' sleep. She sadly needs it. Then she sits up, reads, talks, possibly sews a little (though this is rare), and enjoys life. Towards the end of the afternoon one notices that every right hand is covered with a little bag, out of which the first finger protrudes, and the ladies round one have a preoccupied air. They are telling their beads, which are covered up, inside the little bags. This habit of covering the rosary interests me much, for I am told that the Buddhists of Ceylon, who wear their beads on the right wrist, hide them under a strip of cloth, like the maniple of Christian ritual. No one appears to attach any meaning to the custom.

Some hundreds of the names of God have thus been said—or, as we should put it, the Name has been said some hundreds of times—when dusk falls, and a servant passes the door bearing a lamp. At once all rise and prostrate themselves before some sacred picture in the room, and once more the whole household passes, with various beautiful preliminaries of salutation to the Ganges, to the *tulsi* plant, and so on, to worship, again in the form of meditation. It is the time called candle-light or the hour of peace.

It is quite late before the ladies eat for the second time, and in the pleasant hour or two between, friends and neighbours, attended by female servants bearing lanterns, may slip in for a chat. By half-past nine all have gone, and at ten or shortly after, bathing and supper are alike finished, and everyone retires for the night.

Such is an ideal day for a woman of the upper classes. Where there are no servants, labour has to be carried to its remotest sub-division. One daughter-in-law has charge of all the bread-making; another boils the rice and looks after the potatoes; and so on. And if, in addition to this, there are children, endless ablutions "by drowning in a tank" (to quote a friend's picturesque expression) add to their mother's cares. From early dawn till late at night there is not an idle moment. What a comfort that for us all, the world over—

> "Be the day weary, be the day long,
> At last it ringeth to evensong!"

THE SACRED YEAR

WHETHER or not it is true, as some have held, that all sacred years are built out of the wreckage of more ancient civil years, it is certain beyond any possibility of cavil or question that behind the Hindu sacred year lies another, a weather-year, full of the most loving and delicate observation of nature. Each great day as it comes round is marked by its own particular glinting of sunlight on the leaves, its own rare bite of the morning air, or its own dancing of the blood at noon. When, in the early autumn, the tiny, jonquil-like flowers are found fallen at dawn from the *shephalika* bushes, and the children pick them up blossom by blossom for worship, men say with something of the gladsomeness of childhood itself, "Mother is coming! Mother is coming!" for they remind them of the festival of Durga, by this sign near at hand. In springtime, when the *asoka* tree begins to adorn itself with its bunches of red flowers, that are said never to bud till the tree has heard the footsteps of a beautiful woman, and the long slender buds of the leaf-almond begin to appear, the low castes are glad, for now is coming *Holi*, the Easter of the primitive peoples. On the birthday of Krishna, late in the summer, it *must* rain, in memory of the night so long ago when the Lord of All was carried as a babe, by Vasudeva, through wind and storm. The *Kali Puja*, with its myriads of tiny open lamps, seems always to happen on the night of some marriage-flight amongst the insects, and always the little winged creatures suffer death by fire on these altars of the Mother.

But there is no nature-festival to be compared with that of *Ras*. All through the growing moon of the beautiful month of *Kartik*, the women have gone to the Ganges-side at evening, night after night, with flowers and lamps to offer vows. Now has come the full moon. It is the first of the cold weather. The winter flowers are beginning to bloom. The world is full of relief from the lessening of the long heat. The very trees seem to rejoice in the unwonted coolness, and this was the moment at which Krishna went with the cowherds to the forest. Throughout the rains the cattle have been kept in the villages, and now they are taken to the distant pastures. Oh, the joy of the forests: the long moonlight nights, the whispering trees, the enfolding dark, the presence of the Cowherd, who is in truth the Lord Himself! In those temples which have the necessary buildings the image of Krishna is taken at evening out of its sanctuary, and conveyed in procession to a little Chapel of the Exposition, there to be worshipped publicly until the morning. Here for three days in the small hours of the night, when the moon has scarcely yet begun to wane, come the women to sit and worship, or to go round and round the altar in a circle, silently praying. And choirs of priests chant the while. And the image-sellers drive a brisk though almost silent trade, and the precincts of the temple are thronged with life, imagining itself out in the forest amongst the cowherds, playing with the Lord.

Every full moon has its own special morsel of lore. To-night, at some hour or other, the sweet goddess Lakshmi will enter the room, and we must on no account sleep lest we miss her visit. Again, it is unlucky this month for the heads of the family to see the moon. Therefore they must not look out of the window, and this is well, for to-night is the orchard-robbing festival, when the boys of the village have right to enter the garden and carry off ripe fruit. What wonderful coincidence fixed it to fall when the harvest of the jack-trees is ready for gathering?

The whole of Hinduism is one long sanctification of the common life, one long heart and relating of soul to the world about it; and the love of pilgrimage and the quest of sacred shrines speak of that same desire to commune with nature as the village feasts. The holiness of nature is the fundamental thought of Hindu civilisation. The hardships of life in camp and forest are called austerity; the sight of grass and trees is called worship. And the soothing and peace that come of a glimpse of a great river is held a step on the road to salvation and the freeing of the soul.

How did this passion for nature become fixed and ritualised, in the series of the year's fasts and feasts? Here opens out a field of most fruitful study. A fixed system of universal consent always presupposes some central authority, which persisted long enough not only to pronounce authentically on disputable matters, but also to radiate as custom what had been thus determined. This central authority exists in India as the empire whose seat for nearly a thousand years was Pataliputra.[1] By its rulings was Hinduism, in so far as it is universal throughout the country, shaped and determined, and in order to know exactly what this was in its daily working, it would be necessary to study in

[1] Pataliputra, on the site of the modern Patna, in Behar; capital of the ancient kingdom of Magadha, described by Megasthenes; in the third century B.C. the metropolis of the Emperor Asoka.

detail the worships of Madras and the South. For here we have, more or less in its purity, the Hinduism which grew up, antithetically to Buddhism, during the Buddhist period. It differs in many ways from that of Bengal, since there the faith went through a much longer period of elaboration. Pataliputra was succeeded by Gour, the Guptas by the Sens, and in the year A.D. 728 Adisur Sen, Emperor of the five Gours, as was his title, brought to his capital, and established there for the good of his people in matters of faith and scholarship, the celebrated five Brahmins of Kanauj. And they made the face of Bengal to shine—which is a brief way of saying, probably, that this king established an ecclesiastical college of reference at Gour, which went on impressing its influence on the life of Bengal, long after the original five, and their king, had been gathered to their fathers. Even after the Hindu sovereigns had fallen altogether, and the Mohammedan rulers had taken their place, this Brahminical influence went on living and working. It was in fact the Bengali form of Papacy, and before we rebel against it too much, before we asperse it too bitterly for the cerecloths of orthodoxy which it bound upon the people, we ought to know what were the problems that it had to solve. It gave continuity to the social development of the community, in the face of the most appalling revolutions. It made the faith a strong ground of taste and manners and gave it consciousness of its strength. It made the village into a true civic unit, in spite of complexity of caste and origins. It maintained the growth of literature and the epic-making faculty. And above all—the supreme gift of Hinduism—it went on deepening and widening the education of the people by that form of mind-cultivation which is peculiar to India, the form that she knows not as secular schooling but as devotional meditation, the power to which she will one day owe her recovery, should it be given to her to recover her footing at all, in the world of nations.

The power of the Brahmin was never broken in Bengal till modern education brought new tests to try men by. Mohammedanism had never touched it. The new religion of Chaitanya was not even defiant of it. Automatically it had gone on working and growing. The world is always ready to call any overthrowal of the old by the name of reformation, because in anything long established there is always much that needs overthrow. Pruning and weeding are a parable of necessary processes in thought and society also. But how can we call this a reformation unless we know what new ideals are to be substituted for the old? That destruction has taken place is indisputable, but does destruction alone constitute reformation? In any case, Bengal owes her own solidarity, her unity in complexity, her Hinduistic culture and the completeness of her national assimilation, more perhaps to Adisur and the Brahminical college that he established than to any other single fact of these many centuries.

If this theory be correct, if the wider Hinduistic formalism was the work of the Guptas of Pataliputra, and the orthodoxy of Bengal more especially that of the Sen kings of Gour, a wonderful amount of history lies in the study of the differences between the two. We shall in that case expect to find more ancient and less homogeneous fragments of the faith lying outside of Bengal. We shall look, moreover, to study the development of the popular faith in parallelism with Buddhism outside. For here a long obscuring process has been superposed upon the other. Those elements of Hinduism in which it has marked affinities with the classical and pre-classical religions of Europe must, for the most part, be sought outside, in distant provinces, and at the conservative centres of the great pilgrimage shrines. But for the potentialities of Hinduism, for its power to bind and unite, for its civilising and liberalising effect, we cannot do better than go to Bengal. Here we may disentangle gradually the long story of the influences that have made it what it is. Did the first image-makers come from China? And when? In what order were the main worships introduced? What was the original place of the planetary deities, of snakes and of trees, in the scheme of things? Who were Satya-Pir and Satya-Narayan? These questions, and a thousand like them, have to be answered before we can understand and assign time and source to all the elements that have gone to the making of the *sanatan dharma* in Bengal. Yet wherever we go—north, east, or west—we shall always find that India herself has been the inspiration of Hinduism, and that the faith without the land is a name without a person, a face without a soul.

DOL-JATRA

It was dawn of the beautiful morning that ends the full-moon night of the month of *Phalgun.* In the sick room the light in the small earthen cup flickered and went out, and the cool wind that comes with the first light entered the chamber and fanned with its wings both the watcher and the sick. It was then, in those first rapt moments of sunrise, that there came, from far off by the Ganges side, the sound of the Indian flute, incredibly mysterious and remote, rising and falling in gentle cadences, pausing in sweetness, lingering in tenderness, dominated ever by its own pathos. The music was a hymn of worship, and the night just ended was the birthnight of Chaitanya—Chaitanya, the saint of Nuddea, the poet and emancipator of Bengal. Oh wonderful birth at Nuddea, of the Lover of the People, on the People's Feast! For this full-moon day of *Phalgun* is not only the birthday of Gauranga, but also the *Holi Puja* of the low castes and the *Dol-jatra* of the Hindu calendar.

Whatever else we do not know of the ancient countries, of one thing we may be sure, that in every case they must have had a yearly feast of Eros. We may gather, moreover, from the climatic and geographical associations of each land, the very moon of the festival in every case. It must always have taken place in the spring-time. The memory of this left behind, here a carnival, there a battle of flowers, and somewhere else a May Day frolic, to tell a future age the path it went. Here in India, where all ages persist, like geological strata piled one upon another, it is kept to-day as it may have been in Assyria or Egypt, in early Greece or in the empire of the Hittites.

On full-moon of the beautiful month of *Phalgun*—that month when the *asoka* tree and the mango are in bloom, when the foliage buds of the leaf-almond are long and slender against the blue, and when the scarlet plumes of the *palash* stand out on its naked branches—occurs the *Holi* festival, or *Dol-jatra* of some long pre-Hindu people. Pre-Hindu they certainly were, although Hinduism has done its best to absorb and assimilate the poetry they brought to it. For the *asoka* tree, they say, only blooms when the footfall is heard by it of a beautiful woman, and the fragrance of mango-blossoms is one of the five arrows of Madan's bow—two morsels of the folk-lore that clearly belong to the spring and nature festival. Madan, the Indian Love, is always depicted as a young man, not as a child, who once upon a time went clad in flowers—nay, his very weapon was made of them. And as he wore it loose and unstrung beside his quiver, the eager bees hanging above it gave it its proper form of the bow. So at least we are told in Kalidas's immortal fragment. Wherever Madan is mentioned amongst the educated, Kalidas must needs be remembered, for his was the brain that gave the beautiful young archer his life-myth, and to his poem must all go who would learn of the impious faring forth together of Love and his comrade Spring, to shoot at the heart of the Great God, and of the fate that befell their enterprise in the sacred grove of meditation. All the love of the Indian soil and Indian nature that must have spoken in the wild poetic souls of the earliest aborigines is here poured, together with his own thought and learning, into the crucible of a great Hindu poet, to form the poem of the birth of Kartik the War-Lord. But long before Kalidas took up his lute, the Indian feast of Eros had been Indianized, being interpreted as an incident in the idyll of the sporting of the child Krishna in the meadows of Brindaban. Nothing is so exquisite as this—the tale of the divine childhood as a cowherd amongst the herd-boys and herd-girls beside the Jumna. At the age of eleven Krishna passes off the peasant stage for ever, but years after, when his forest-friends visit him in his palace, they refuse to recognise their old playmate whom they now see in kingly robes, and will not be satisfied till he has donned once more for them his childhood's crown of a peacock's feather, with flute and simple village garments, thus revealing himself again to their adoring love as the same Gopala they knew of old.

Everyone who knows anything of the village customs of the North-West has seen the place that swinging holds in the Indian peasant's conception of a festival. Boys and girls, young men and young women, like English rustics at a fair, swing and shout, applaud and deride each other, with never a suggestion of that dignity which we commonly associate with Oriental humanity. It is wonderful how easily, with a rope and a few bamboos and a wooden seat, a swing can be made for a frolic. But in the Himalayas, near every temple, we find swing-posts of deodar and stout iron chains. Clearly there was a time when the festival was celebrated everywhere, and since Brindaban must so obviously have known the giddy delight, it followed that a swinging ceremony became part of the religious ritual of the altar on the day of the Spring Feast. In other words, Hinduism, by means of the Krishna legend, had absorbed into itself, and in doing so, lent a greater dignity of interpretation to, the Festival of Love of the country folk.

Hinduism absorbed, Hinduism reinterpreted,

but she never criticised or discountenanced the gaiety of the child races. And still the lower castes maintained the old practices of the season. There are perhaps two essential elements characteristic of the festivals of Madan. One is the free mixing of men and women, with probably a certain element of rough buffoonery, something like the old St. Valentine's Day of Europe; and the other, the drawing together of all the classes, ignoring social differences of higher civilisations of later ages. These two characteristics have persisted to the present day in the *Holi Puja* observances of the Hindu lower classes, and Hindu gentlefolk of mature age will tell how in their childhood their mothers would bend the head to receive the red-powder *tilaka* at the hands of their Hindustani servants.

Out in the streets meanwhile the boys are at war with passing pedestrians, all of whom are bound on this privileged day to submit to being pelted with red powder. Yellow powders are sometimes used, but this, say the best judges, is a mistake. The red alone is correct, symbolising the sand of the Jumna, all stained with the blood of the demons, whom Krishna slew. The wild and boisterous, impatient of the priest's slow blessing, buy the powder straight from shops and throw it. But gentler spirits wait, playing only with that which is duly offered and sanctified in worship.

And great is the reward of their patience, for such is the virtue of the blest powder that it confers immunity, it is said, from all diseases of the season!

Here then in India to this day is played out every year the old-time drama of the peasant in the spring; played, too, in a fashion of which, however it may annoy the Philistine, neither the scholar nor the poet could bear to sacrifice a single point. The joy of simple peoples in the bridal of nature, and the festival of the great democracy of caste and sex—these are two impulses that have given birth to all carnivals and *Holi Pujas* that the world has ever known. And behind, watching over them, suggesting a thought of poetry here, a touch of sanctity there, and working to moderate possible excess only by her own benign presence and her kindly tolerance, stands the ancient Mother-Church of Hinduism. There was a wonderful dramatic fitness in the fact that in the fulness of time it was on the full-moon of *Phalgun*, the day of the *Holi* festival, that Chaitanya, apostle of rapture, lover of the poor and lowly, the national saint and the preacher of democracy, was born here in Bengal.

JANMASTAMI: THE DAY OF THE GREAT BIRTH

A SUDDEN chime of bells, a blaze of lights waved before an altar—while without, the watching stars and purple blackness of the midnight sky look down—such is the solemn moment of the Birth of Krishna.

Surely it is only in this country, where a temple perforce takes the form of a verandah, that Nature wholly mingles herself with worship, to bring the sense of the Divine to man. The Western monk chants his Hours—Lauds and Prime and Matins, and Terce and Sext and Vespers and Nones—but those footfalls of the Sun that he commemorates were trodden long ago in the deserts of the Thebaid, and he sings within closed doors, holding himself snug against the chill winds without. Here in India, however, we practise the Faith in the very land, and every day we realise afresh the cosmic events that gave it birth. Who has felt the stillness that falls on lawn and river at the moment of noon? Who, watching through long hours, has heard the distant music of the flute arise by the Ganges side with the first ray of dawn? Who has wandered in field and forest at the time of cowdust, and known the sudden touch of twilight on the soul, without understanding why the village bells ring and prayers are enjoined at the stated hours? For that which in one man's eyes is superstition, another may know to be but an added firmness of sensation. But surely of all the worships in the Hindu cycle, none has the power and force of those celebrated at midnight. When slumber has fallen on men, gathered together in the great hive of Night; when even the wild creatures are still, each in his place on hillside or bough; when all that is trivial and personal has been blotted out with the passing of the sunlight, till, in the sound of the river, we can almost hear that of the far-off sea—then the lamps of the altar shine as though they were in truth the heart of the universe; then the worshipper feels himself to be but one of an innumerable host of stars and worlds, all of which wait with him for the dawn in the darkness of Light Ineffable. And most of all this is true of the midnight service of the Birth of Krishna.

Among the higher castes in Bengal it is customary that each house shall contain a private chapel of its own, and only the poor and the lowly betake themselves to temples for the observance of the great festivals; but to my own household, perhaps as a proof of our perversity of disposition, this is rather a reason for frequenting them than otherwise. We love to see the band of simple worshippers, for the most part women, who arrive now and again and seat themselves to watch the ceremony in the outer court, while an elderly priest gives informal religious instruction during the preliminary stages of the function. We like, too, to listen to that religious instruction itself, and to the questions which now and again it has to meet. And so one night we sat on the steps of a certain temple of Kali, which stands at a corner hard by and looks far across the Ganges with the hay boats drawn up in line beneath the bank, on and on to the edge of the world in the distant North-West. The temple is old, and the corner rounded off with the wisdom and beauty peculiar to the old Indian method of laying out a town, and the image that dwells there, under a sheltering *bo*-tree, is known as "the Kali of the Hay-merchants." Only a few years ago the spot was at the extreme end of Calcutta, but to-day this can no longer be said, though there is still a large open space opposite, where a great tree stands, and now and then gives a long shivering cry, as if to warn the neighbourhood of coming storm.

All the evening through the street had been full of passers up and down. And sudden bursts of singing and sounding of *shankh* and gongs had disturbed the ordinary quiet in all directions. For we are early old-fashioned folk in the Hindu quarter of Calcutta. Lights are out and noises hushed, as a rule, before ten o'clock; and by eleven o'clock, even on the Janmastami, everything was closed except the temples. Here, by the light of his own altar, an Uriya priest still sat chanting the tale of the Holy Birth from a palm-leaf book. There, a few Brahmins chatted late round the foot of an image at which presently they would be offering worship. But the bamboo mats were all up and padlocked in front of the shops, and only the lamplights from the open shrines streamed across the curb.

It was thus that we waited for the moment of the Birth. The temple had disappeared. The tones of the kindly old priest sounded dim and far away. Centuries had rolled back. The walls of a prison closed about us, and we waited once more with the royal victims, Devaki the mother and Vasudev the father, for the coming of the Holy Child. Once more, as on the first Day of the Birth, the rains seemed to fall and the winds to blow, and the only sound that reached us besides the violence of the storm was the heavy breathing of the guards, smitten into slumber by spirits, carrying to the prison of Kangsa the commission of the Most High. Surely never was the anguish of motherhood so great as on that night! Seven times had Devaki given life, and seven times had it been snatched away by the cruel king her brother, as soon as given—for had it not been told that one of her babes should be his enemy and take his life? And now at the coming of the eighth child, especially named in the prophecy, and looked for with concentrated passion of fierceness and jealousy—how, in that seven-times wounded heart, could there be room for joy?

Heavy moments are these, full of bitterest anguish of expectancy and dread; full of the agony of love that longs to save, but finds no means for protection of the Beloved, and yet at the same time moments in which is mingled a sense of lofty faith, a growing awe, an intuition of infinite tenderness and triumph.

It was over at last. Before them lay the Babe Himself, all laughter, all radiance. One more had been added to the "wretched births" of the Avataras, and even in a prison the mystery of Incarnation made itself felt.

The books say that it was the new-born child who instructed Vasudev to wrap him in his cloak, and pass out of the prison to the village on the far side of the Jumna, and then substitute him for the new-born girl of Nanda the cowherd and return. Was it so, indeed? Or was it overwhelming clearness of vision that came with the presence of the Divine and seemed like speech?

However that be, it met with prompt and eager obedience from the royal prisoners. No mother's weakness of Devaki, no masculine scepticism of Vasudev, was put forward to check for one moment the course of events. Concealing under his mantle the shining Child, the father turned to make his way through darkness and storm. The guards slept soundly; the prison doors opened silently of their own accord. And none had ever seen the Lord of the Worlds save him who carried Him. Terrible was the storm, and full of terror the flood of the Jumna when the moment came for crossing it. Here and there Vasudev tried, but it was impossible to find means, when suddenly a jackal passed in before him, and he, guided by this lowliest of beasts, forded the stream in safety and reached the hut of Nanda the cowherd. Here, too, sound sleep had fallen upon all, and Yasoda herself, when she awoke in the morning, did not know that the Boy in her arms was a changeling, nor dreamed that he was in truth of the royal house.

In the prison, however, a terrible scene had been enacted. The infuriated sovereign, Kangsha, informed of the occurrence at last of the long-expected birth, had come in person to visit the prisoners. Suspecting foul play when he saw a female child, but unable to substantiate his suspicions, he seized the infant by the feet to dash it to pieces against the wall. But the girl was an incarnation of Yogmaya, and the king suddenly found his clenched fingers empty, while over above him, illuminating the chamber with her glow, stood the great Goddess. "Your enemy is even now growing to manhood," she said, "in the village of the cowherds," and then the vision faded out and there was none with them.

Poor fate-maddened king—doomed by each act only to fill deeper the cup of his iniquities till the destined champion should appear, and in single combat avenge the wrongs of his people and his blood—how sad and yet how necessary was the part that he played in the story of Brindaban and the wondrous childhood! How strange—but at this point a movement among the priests interrupted our memories and recalled us to the present. The mystical moment of midnight had come. The Holy Child was born once more among men, and here, not in a prison but in a temple, and amidst the music of bells, with flowers, and lights, and incense, we were to celebrate that old-time coming of the Lord of Worlds. Many minutes passed in silence and prostration, and then we slipped away through the chime-broken hush of the quiet street to our own door.

But as we reached it we lingered for a moment

regretfully on the threshold. "Ah surely," said we, "this is no accustomed scene. For in truth we have come through wind and storm across the Ju'mna, and, bearing the Holy Babe beneath our cloak, we are but now arrived at the hut of Nanda the cowherd in the village of Gokul."

THE SARASWATI PUJA

We realise too little that the world's greatest images and temples are but as mountain-peaks, in which culminate the private adorations of the soul and of the home. Out of the spoils of Marathon, Athene Promachos was set to watch, from the rocky summit of the Acropolis, over the city of violets, only because, beside the hearths of Athens, for more than two centuries before the time of Pheidias, her name had been a household word. But if we would know something of that long anterior thought and dreaming that made her and the Goddess of the Parthenon what they have become to us and to our children, we cannot do better than study the question here in Bengal, in the simple worships of the months as they go by. For Greece in her golden age, though politically emancipated, was intellectually but a province of Asia, and in Hindu India to-day that same Asia is still alive and in full vigour. Pater's Roman study of Marius the Epicurean, laying his violets and cake with the fragment of honeycomb on the votive shelf before the tablets of his ancestors and of the gods, would apply with precision to the Bengali woman of this present year of grace, offering *prasadam* and flowers, with grass and water, before the household deity in her *thakur-ghar*. The *thakur-ghar*, or private oratory, is sufficient for the needs of the daily worship of the family. But when the great *pujas* come round the image is erected downstairs, in the hall that runs along the side of the front court—the noblest apartment in the house—and the whole dwelling falls into subordination as a temple of the gods.

Man has had many dreams of the Divine Wisdom, but surely few so touching as this of Saraswati in Bengal. A simple woman, ascetic and poor, standing on the white lotus, surrounded by flowers, not jewels, suggestive of all things white and colourless and simple, and carrying the mystic Vina, from which the touch of her hand is bringing a secret music—this is she who has been our guest. In the Dekkan and in Maharashtra, they picture her riding on the peacock, and Mhattre's beautiful statue, with its decorative draperies and crown-like hair, carries not a little splendour with it. But in Bengal the goddess is somewhat widowlike—not actually a widow, for among her offerings is the iron bracelet of the wife—true daughter of the ascetics and patron of poor students, impossible to confound with Lakshmi, her sister of Good Fortune.

Seeing it for the first time at sunset or at dawn, one learns to appreciate the dainty curves of the image: the gleaming white, the light and springing attitude, as of one scarcely touching the flower on which she stands. But it is not even necessary to have an image in order to worship Saraswati. It is quite sufficient, instead, to set one's inkstand and pens in her hallowed place, and offer to them our salutation and affection. For Saraswati dwells and is found in these, the humble creatures of learning; and in token thereof—in full accord with the Hindu horror of confounding use and worship—her worshippers are forbidden to open a book or touch their writing materials throughout her festival.

A world of childish associations and tender joys lies hidden beneath the observance of the *Saraswati Puja*. Kind uncles and fathers stay at home to-day, and prove the value of leisured masculinity by their readiness to ascend step-ladders and nail the auspicious strings of mango-leaves above the entrance, and carry pots of water and place them, covered with cocoanuts, and embowered beneath tall plantain-stems, against portals and pillars everywhere. And the children themselves are all hilarity. To hold hammer and nails, or carry flowers and mats, seems the height of glory. In the kitchen the ladies of the house are busy preparing food and dressing many-coloured fruits. The happy bustle of an English Christmas prevades the household, all to culminate in the solemn worship, about noon, when the Austere Spirit of Learning will be invoked, and implored to make this hospice of her two-days' visitation her home and abode throughout the coming year.

In the making of the altar-place itself, how much to do! First must the place be cleansed and sanctified. Then, on a wooden stand, the image is set up and all the necessary appurtenances of Saraswati's manifestation arranged about her in due order. Reed pens of an ancient make, curious earthen ink-wells, of no modern pattern, a quaint toilet-basket, with combs and scented oils, a small round mirror, and powders and earthenware vessels innumerable, are all *de rigueur* on this occasion. Let priests and theologians explain the mirror how they will, as symbolising the reflection of the Divinity in the unclouded mind, or *buddhi* —it strikes the newcomer very forcibly that, in sentiment at least, the goddess is to some extent a lady visitant, to whom the privileges and courtesies of womanhood must be extended; for whom, indeed, her sister-women will think many luxuries necessary that they could by no means afford for themselves. Last, and most striking, perhaps, of the preliminary ceremonies is the enclosing of the sacred space. Balls of mud are set at the four corners. In these are placed arrows with the points downwards, and then—in the case of Saraswati white, in that of other images red—thread is passed from corner to corner, a palisade of cord and arrows. Under what conditions of forest and hunt were the Hindu images first set up for worship?

The name Saraswati occurs in the Vedas themselves, and we can gather its primitive significance from the fact that it was applied to that river on whose banks were performed all the holiest sacrifices. The word is a synomym also for Savitri, which is one of the names of the Gayatri, or national prayer. So that in a very special sense it is said by Hindus of this, their Divine Wisdom, that she is the eternal consort of the Creator, and sprang, full-grown, from the countenance of Narayan, the Lord of the Worlds. "O Thou without Whom the Creator Himself abideth not, abide with us!" runs one of the prayers, and the enumeration that follows of the eight-fold desirable attributes of the mind is curiously subtle. A distinction is drawn, for instance, between memory and the power to call up the thing remembered at the right time and place.

There is, humanly speaking, understood to be a silent unyielding grudge between Saraswati and her sister Lakshmi, the Mistress of Fortune. To be entirely abandoned by Lakshmi is a terrible curse. It means to become devoid of all beauty and charm of every kind: to be, in the world of men, as an owl hooting in the wilderness. Even Saraswati, too, must have recourse to the good offices of Lakshmi for that measure of oats and midnight oil which is the essential wealth of the poor student. But it would be foolish to look, in the case of either sister, for the bestowal of the fulness of her benediction on the ardent adorer of the other. Each is very jealous, and gives herself completely only to a whole heart and an undivided affection. Especially is it true of this plainly-garbed Mother, throned on the white lotus, that she stands in right queenly strength on her own simplicity, and grants but the crumbs of her feast to him who has a squinting regard for the good things of life's banquet. How quietly thus, in a half-sarcastic myth, has India foretold the disaster to learning that would come of modern commercialism! The lore of Saraswati has other points of significance. All books and manuscripts—Persian and English to the full as much as classic Sanskrit—are sacred to her. We find plenty of science and geography among the school-books that the boys place on her altar shyly, to be blessed by the touch of her feet. There is no suspicion in India of divorce between faith and knowledge, between the Divine Creator and the Divine Wisdom. The thing sounds foolish. Is not religion the highest knowledge, knowledge itself the highest faith?

Thus we gather that there is in Hinduism full sanction for the difficult intellectual transition through which the present generations are passing. The Mother blesses that absorption in intellectual problems that forgets her name. She accepts such oblivion as the most precious form of worship. But it must be the pursuit of knowledge for the sake of knowledge, not for that of its loaves and fishes. Those of us who have learned to regard the present Indian crisis as one almost entirely of mind and thought will realise the dynamic power of these conceptions. For on no other terms than those of a complete appropriation of new forms of disinterested culture can the nation hope to take its true place in the modern world. And to such an excursion of the intellect its ancient sources of authority offer full encouragement and benediction. Without any break with her own past, India might learn to stand in the very van of modern progress. Some understanding of such facts, more or less dim, penetrates even the humblest household in which the image of Saraswati is set up. What is lacking is a sense of contrast, the knowledge that in such a breadth of view there is anything startling or extraordinary.

Saraswati in modern India is the favourite goddess of every home, even as Athene must have been in almost prehistoric Athens. But the altar of Athene was the cradle of a great civic life and organisation, and the throne of Saraswati has up to the present inculcated only an invisible culture —mediæval in its intensity—of heart and soul. Treasures of Indian psychology, treasures of Indian thought, lie scattered by the roadside for him who cares to follow out with attention the winding paths of Hindu worship. Yet none who has watched the procession of the image to the river can doubt that the Indian *pujas* of to-day, like the Greek of old, contain within themselves great civic possibilities.

For the two days, with their constant succession of sacred offices, are gone. All night long the lights burned about the shrine, and long after evenfall an occasional passer-by, noting the garland of leaves above the entrance, would push open the door and enter the courtyard to spend a few moments in the presence of the altar. Ever since the consecration of the image we have gone about on tiptoe and spoken almost in whispers, feeling that the house was not our own, but the dwelling-place of gods. And now the second evensong is come, and after the pathetic ceremony of the Farewell Charge is done among the women, the goddess goes forth, amidst attendant drums and heralds, to disappear from the eyes of mortals in that flood wherein all that is is holy. Crowded streets and river-bank await her coming, and even as the one procession goes out it meets another coming in, bearing the pots of Ganges water from which in the growing dusk the "water of peace" will be sprinkled on kneeling worshippers, while the last blessings are pronounced in the chamber where for two days she had stood. How exquisite is this moment of "the water of peace"; how full of devotion are prayers and prostrations! And among the lengthening shadows there steals about us the sense of something more real than physical presence, and we wonder if to us also has come some of the fruit of the ancient prayer to the Divine Wisdom, "O Thou without whom the Creator Himself abideth not, abide with us!"

THE DURGA PUJA

"AND there was war in Heaven: Michael and his angels fought against the Dragon; and the Dragon fought and his angels, and prevailed not, neither was their place found any more in Heaven." Archaic sentences here and there in the world's scriptures tell us of the wars that were waged in Heaven before the beginning of time, and of the heritage—dim, prehistoric, supernatural in the natural—that was left from them to men and gods.

What is it that makes this element of mythology so clear, what force has raised it in this one case to the significance which it attains in the *Chandi* portion of the *Markandeya Purana?* This is, above all others, the *Purana* of Bengal. But here the central figure of the drama is no archangel, mighty in power and beauty, but the Mother herself, personification of the creative energy, focus and centre of the visible Universe. Back and forth amidst the applause of Heaven does She pursue the ever-changing demons, and at the moment of her triumph, when, ten-armed, pedestaled on the living lion and sword in hand, She subjugates her foe for ever, She is portrayed as the image of Durga. Such is the story told by the scripture—half-epic, half-liturgy—from which are taken the texts that are recited over and over again from one end of Bengal to the other, with worship and fasting, throughout the great nine days, from the new moon of *Aswin*, until *Dussera* or tenth day. Here and there are those—monks in their monasteries, perhaps, or Brahmins in their homes—who recite the whole of the *Chandi* again and again. But for all alike, whether they do this or not, there is but one object of contemplation—the wars that were in Heaven; one hope, and one alone—the conquest of the demons by the gods.

Everywhere in India the feast that corresponds to the *Durga Puja* is military in character. Perhaps fundamentally in consequence of the fact that, in the North at least, the rains are just over, the first seven days are spent in the cleaning and display of weapons; and on the tenth occurs the prostration and exhibition of skill in arms. Very curious is it at Nagpur on this day to see the last scion of the Bhonslas set out on the stately promenade that was, to his fathers, the beginning of a freebooting expedition, and long long before that, a hunting party.

But domestically, in Bengal, it is a very different element in the festival that determines the feeling of the home with regard to it. The child to whose after life each flash of a waterfall is to carry its reminder, more or less vivid, of Durga with crown and sword, does not in its childhood itself conceive of Her as the cosmic energy, appearing from amidst the ten points of the compass. For the Mother of the Universe shines forth in the life of humanity as a woman, as family life, and as country. Here She is the maiden, perfect in beauty, nun-like in holiness, whose past and future are a glorified wifehood, on whose rapture of devotion the eye of the Great God Himself has fallen, and who enters the Indian household, goddess and queen notwithstanding, as, after all, the little wedded daughter, returning for a ten-days' visit to her father's house.

True, as the lad draws nearer to manhood, he must realise that the father of the guest is no less than Himalaya, and his daughter, therefore, the spouse of God—according to the legend, Mother India herself. But this only gives continuity and ductility to his idea of the myth. First Durga, the ten-days visitant; secondly, India, as Uma Haimavati; and lastly, Maha-Sakti, the Infinite Force: but always and increasingly as his power of recognition grows, that ceaseless energy which works without and around him towards the due subordination, by the forces of life and nature, of all that is vicious and unjust and out of place.

With what tenderness and intimacy, then, does the Bengali child learn to conceive of his country and of God! It is a tenderness and intimacy which, beginning with the use of images, may become inherent in a language and characteristic of old races. The Mohammedan boatman of Eastern Bengal is not in his own person a worshipper of Durga, and yet the words "With folded hands before the Mother" may carry as much to him as to the Hindu heart. Beyond a doubt, however, it is its higher theological meaning which lends to the *Durga Puja* its overwhelming elements of civic pageantry and national comprehensiveness. Those who have studied religions as factors in social and political development must be conscious of the great variety of threads that are united in any single religious practice. What was it that made the Semitic races worshippers of God the Father, and India the land of the worship of the Mother? Can these vast tangles of social and geographical conditions ever be completely unravelled? And even so, does India stand alone in her personification, or is it not more or less common to the whole of Eastern Asia? Regarding this last point, it is perhaps the fact that what exists elsewhere in fragments and survivals has been preserved and developed in India as a coherent whole. And within India itself, customs and doctrines bearing on this worship, in more or less of mutual un-relation, in many provinces, are in Bengal gathered together and woven into a single perfect piece. Who shall say how old was the *Chandi* in this region when it was fitted into and accounted for, by the *Markandeya Purana?* And where can we go, outside the province, that some echo of the old-time Mother-worship does not fall upon our ear?

Aman, the Mother, guards every village of the South. It was Bhowani, the terrible Mother, who led the Mahrattas to victory. The Mother, again, was worshipped by the Sikh, using his sword as her image. Kali was the patron goddess of Chitore. To this day the great birthday is marked, in the Punjab and throughout the North-West Provinces, by the *Ram-Lilla*, or miracle play of the Ramayana. To this day, in Mysore and all over the Dekkan, *Dussera Puja* is the chief festival of the year. To this day, in every part of India, the nine-days fast is performed by some member of every high-caste household. To this day, in Madras, in Behar, and among families of military tradition everywhere, is Virashtamy, the solemn eighth day, the occasion of the worship and the tribute of the sword.

In Bengal, however, all these elements—social, military, and theological—are combined and rationalised in the characteristic conception of the Divine Mother as Durga-Kali-Jagadhattri:

Durga, the divine energy, making and destroying, defeated and again conquering, impersonal and indifferent to personal desires; Kali, mother of darkness, wielder of destruction, receiver of sacrifice, whose benediction is death; and, finally, Jagadhattri, the tenderness of the heart of God, who shines in good women, and from whom came forth the Madonnas of the world. It is in Bengal, too, when the image of the Mother has left her children for a space, when the nine days of worship and of charity are ended; it is in Bengal that the great tenth day is kept as that of the reknitting of human ties, and the *bijoya* greetings of the family reunion go out throughout the length and breadth of the land. For are not all bonds of kindred indeed sanctified and renewed year by year at the feet of the Divine Visitant? Is not the whole of the country at one in the presence of the Mother?

It is more than thirty years since Bankim Chandra Chatterji, the great Bengali romancer, sang the vision of the ended *Durga Puja* as the hour of the Motherland's need as he saw the image plunge beneath the waves. That the poet spoke the innermost thought of his countrymen, interpreting the yearly drama that belongs to each one in a national sense, however distant he may be in the sectarian; that he voiced in his poem what each household and each individual had known already in the heart, is proved by the history that has gathered round his song. Every year that goes by, the images of the Mother become more and more deeply, each in its turn, entwined with the thought of India to the Indian heart. Mother and Motherland—where ends the one and where begins the other? Before which does a man stand with folded hands, when he bows his head still lower, and says with a new awe: "My Salutation to the Mother!"

THE FESTIVAL OF RAS

HIGH to the south shone Orion, as, a couple of hours before dawn, on the second day after the full moon of November, we opened the great doors of the house and went forth into the silent lane. About us was the quiet of midnight. The moon, so little waned, made the black sky seem blacker, and the bright stars brighter, and in the air was a touch of wintry cold. Now and then, as we pressed onward to the temple, a couple of women, veiled and muffled, would pass us hurriedly, their bare feet as they struck the earth making still less sound than our own. The path was narrow by which, at last, we must tread our way into the temple-precincts. The court formed a parallelogram, giving, through an arch at its further end, upon the street. To right and left its sides were formed of long rows of buildings. The entrance to the temple itself, the hall of worship, was at some distance in the wall upon our right. And here, at the approach, the near end was almost closed by a small circular building, a sort of domed arcade, lifted high above the level of the ground and surrounded by a procession path, with stairs to the right and left.

This was in fact the chapel of the exposition, standing open, silent, and empty, the year round. This morning, however, it was not empty: for on the altar beneath its dome stood the images, throned on flowers, of Radha and Krishna, brought there in procession from the sanctuary, some time after midnight. And without, on the stairs and terrace of the ambulatory, a line of quiet women circulated, their bowed heads and wrapt faces, or the beads half-hidden beneath their veils, telling of the worship in which they were absorbed. Even in the distance, outside the narrow precincts, the sight of these women doing *pradakshina* gave a feeling of unwonted stir. But nothing could have prepared us for the sight that greeted us as we actually entered. The whole court was ablaze with light. Inside square enclosures made of rope two separate choirs were seated on the ground, chanting the litanies to the accompaniment of stringed instruments. The walls right and left were lined with scores of little booths, where small religious images, household utensils, and a great assortment of baskets, were being bought and sold. And between the two, between devotees and traffickers, were coming and going hundreds of women. Here and there, in some corner in the shadow, would be found one seated alone and lost in prayer ; and high on the plinth, on a level with our heads, the quiet procession of worshippers went on, ascending to join the line by one stair, and leaving it to mingle with the crowd by the other. But down here, on the floor of the court, one met widows and family parties—mothers and their daughters, girls and their companions, threading their way, their worship done, from point to point ; staying here and there to chat a moment with some friend, or pausing at the stalls to chaffer over their wares, and perhaps to buy a toy or a gift for someone at home. The crowd was constantly growing by the addition of newcomers, and as constantly being depleted by the loss of those who were drifting off for bathing to the Ganges side, or turning to go home. Within half an hour of dawn the precincts would be deserted. By night the images would be reinstalled amidst the shadows of their sanctuaries. For the present, however, all was piety and gentle gaiety. Outside, the fading moon smiled down upon the sleeping city. Nothing seemed to be moving beneath the folds of darkness. Yet here, within the little space of brilliant lamplight, buzzed the crowd of graceful well-born women. Here was day before daylight, in a world apart—a woman's world, whose very existence one sleeping a stone's throw off might never have suspected.

How well has Hinduism understood how to

provide opportunities, that each of her children, even her cloistered secluded womanhood, may feast on the changing circling beauties of the year! In all the round of months, no other full moon is held so beautiful as this, the first of the winter season. The rains are over; the festival of Durga, the Mother, is past; and now begins the out-of-doors life of forest and pasture. This was the time at which the Lord Krishna—living among the cowherds on the bank of the Jumna—went forth, with the herdsmen and herdswomen of Gokul, taking their cattle to the meadows of Brindaban. At this time of year began that wondrous life—of play and conquest, of constant self-sacrifice and easy victory—that is, in fact, the idyll of the Indian peasant, the epos of the Indian Herakles. In every woodland at this time of year may be heard, by the inner ear, the music of the Divine Flute-player. Out of any bush might peep the laughing face of the Holy Child, beneath its crown of peacocks' feathers. Mothers and maids have a reverence for all play: for He, the Lord, plays through these winter months in the forests round Gokul!

Three evenings ago, when the moon was full, the images were carried from temple to tabernacle at the hour of sunset with all the men of the village in procession behind them. Thus was dramatised the idea of the cowherds going forth.

All night long the priests watched and served, and at midnight began the women's worship. The Divine Cowherd was dwelling now in the pasture-lands, and they came, as it were, to visit and adore. The next night the exposition began at two, and to-day it was opened at four. All these three dawns have been sacred to the women, and at eight o'clock this morning the festival will be over. But in rich mens' gardens along the Ganges banks a special devotion may prolong it to a week, a fortnight, or a month. Each day, long before sunrise, the images will be carried to their throne of flowers, and there, beneath the sky, their visitors will worship them and spend hours of prayer that is more like play with the Herdsmen of Souls, tending his cows as in the forest at Brindaban.

A little while and our feast will have vanished, for this year, into the past. But in truth a note has been sounded for pious souls in whose key the winter will be pitched. To mother and wife, will not the thought of any one of her beloved be as a glimpse caught of the Divine Cowherd—now spouse of the soul, and again the laughing, playing human babe? Is there any impulse or memory of sweetness that is not like the sound of his flute, calling suddenly across the meadows? Oh, when that note is heard, how eager should be the feet that haste to answer, along the forest paths in the secret places of the heart!

"When his flute calls," says a song of the people, "I must be ready! Early or late, easy or hard, no matter, I must go; and go, let the way through the forest be thorny when it sounds. I spread thorns every day on the courtyard floor, that on them I may learn to walk. And lest in the rains I should hear his call, I throw water where I am to step. For when He calls me I must hasten, and on the way I must not slip."

How foolish are those who dream that *Ras Mela* comes but once a year, and ends! To the eyes of the wise man life itself is that forest on the banks of the Jumna in which ever dwells the Lord, filling sweet days with mirthful labour, and calling the soul from height to height of hidden joy.

THE PLAGUE

"I HAVE a case for you, Sister." It was the doctor's voice in the doorway, and I knew at once what he meant. My first case of plague. A few minutes later we entered the cottage where the patient lay. It was an ordinary mud hut, with its tiny unlighted compartments opening on a central court. In one room lay a quantity of clean linen, for the people were *dhobies;* in another division was the family cow; and at the moment of our entrance the matter in hand was the lifting of the invalid out of a confined room to a small wooden bed on the veranda. Utterly lethargic he lay there, poor child, a bright promising boy of twelve or fourteen. He had been ill since the previous evening; it was now nine o'clock in the morning; the bubo was slightly developed; and with the gravest predictions and repeated instructions the doctor hurried off to attend just such another.

It was so little that could be done. Food, medicine, and a bath—all these could be given. Yes, and the head could be shaved, ice applied, and a fan kept going; but when all was said and done, one was sitting there to watch a human being die—to watch, without hope of saving. For no one who knew the awful intensity of the struggle into which he would presently have to enter, who knew too the overgrown and underfed condition of the child himself, could have a doubt as to the way the battle would end. The evening would come, and he would die. So the doctor had said. Not that I realised this. If I had, I doubt whether I could have driven the mother off at once, as, to my bitter regret, I did, possessed by the notion that isolation and disinfection, the only services I could render, should be thoroughly performed. She was busy near her boy, fanning him perhaps, and constantly inhaling the air that he was breathing out. Did I know she was his mother? I should like to think not. I should like to make any excuse for the fact that I pointed out to her that it would be wise if she sat some distance away. Poor mother! She went at once, crushed and broken-spirited, without a word. But quietly, quietly the tears began to flow down her poor thin face, and she broke into stifled sobs. That was too much. I found something that she must do, and with careful advice brought her back to do it. And there she sat, thenceforward, curled up beside the pillow with the boy's head at her feet.

He was violent now, and the great effort was to keep him quiet, for one unlucky movement might be fatal. But even in his delirium I had this always before me—the sight of perfect love between a mother and her son. Once, indeed, mistaking me for her, he snatched at my hand, and carried his own to his lips, and often, not catching his mother's eyes, he would smile at me—always with that same debonair and tender look of the good comrade, given to carrying the burdens and bringing his mother cheer. I was reminded of that moment earlier in the morning, when he had caught the announcement that no barber could be got for him under two or three pice, and struggling to rise from his bed had cried that he would bring him for one.

He was evidently a good boy, in more senses than one—a devotee and a dreamer of dreams. For every now and then, as a gleam of consciousness would displace the awful look of alienation in the great brown eyes—every now and then he would call loudly upon *Shiva, Kali!* or repeat words of worship; and nothing soothed and quieted him like the incessant repetition of *Haribol*, or the hymn that was commonly sung about the streets at that time:

"Call on the Lord,
Call on the Lord,
Call on the Lord, my brother,

Than this name of the Lord,
For mortal man,
There is no other way."

"There is no other way," the weak voice would murmur in snatches after me, and then the invisible hand would again, as it were, draw the curtain, and the soul would be seen no more at the windows whence for a moment it had looked forth.

And so the end came. All day long the family had watched in the courtyard, his mother and myself on the little veranda. All day long they had been eager to serve in every way that was possible, and when I had to go away for an hour or two my place was taken by a young man from the neighbourhood, whose quiet dignity and firmness in dealing with the patient roused my hearty admiration. At five in the afternoon the doctor returned. "He is getting very low," he said; "another hour or two at most and the outburst will end in a collapse of the heart."

How long the minutes seemed! For the last outbreak of violence was very short-lived, and ended in a wild attempt to repeat the *Haribol* for a length of time. I took up the words, and stood saying them over and over to the movements of the fan, while with a look of relief the lad's head sank back on the pillow. He lay quiet, the breath came in shorter and shorter gasps, and he died.

"Give me twelve instead of one," said the doctor, "and I can try steam baths."

It was evident that one could hope to do nothing alone. All the medical men held that a man once down with plague was doomed. It was a great thing to know that there was a field for work; that the disease, though so deadly, was neither repulsive nor specially infectious; that assistance was wanted in order to try finer methods of treatment; and above all, that, as I had ample opportunity of verifying later, no prejudice of caste or religion would stand in the way of our help being accepted. But in order to act upon all this knowledge, religious orders like those Franciscans of the Middle Ages who put an end to the same disease in Europe would be required, so for the moment we gave up the idea.

Then persons with influence were consulted, and offers of help came from zenana ladies, if we should turn a house of our own into a women's hospital. At this point our difficulties began to be amusing. The nurses were to be zenana ladies, and so were the patients. This sounded simple enough. But the latter would insist on being accompanied to the hospital by their husbands, brothers, or sons, who would watch by their bedside day and night. And in that case, how could the nurses attend to them?

"Besides," said the kindly official who was advising us, "to turn your house into a hospital would involve some little expense, and do you know what would be your chance of receiving patients, after all?"

I shook my head.

"There are more than six hundred hospitals in Calcutta,"[1] he said, "and they contain an aggregate of something like four patients."

So our dream of a hospital for Bengali women, managed by Bengali ladies, also came to an end, and we also realised the wisdom of the Government in deciding that its duty lay not in grappling with the disease itself, but rather with the conditions that had led to its development.

The conditions which are immediately preventible appear to be twofold: (1) insanitation, and (2) ignorance; and if solid work is done towards the removal of these evils, it cannot but be that the plague shall prove a friend to mankind in the long run.

One of its first and greatest services has lain in the humanising of the lower castes. Their labour is at this moment in high demand. Bright little sweeper-boys command the wages of full-grown men, with short hours and plenty of encourage-

[1] Six hundred hospitals was a computation that included all family hospitals and single rooms licensed and set apart as wards under the Plague Regulations. Even of these many were allowed to lapse, so that the actual number came to be much below six hundred while still unnecessarily large. [This refers to the outbreak of 1899.]

ment and stimulus to work. How proud of themselves the conservancy gangs look, spades in their hands and buckets on their shoulders! Strange how all things work in together to further the great purpose of an epoch, and even a catastrophe like the present is really to hasten that supreme function of the English in India, the giving of democracy to the Indian people. For the immediate outcome of good work and good wages is sure to be the establishment of schools in sweeper-villages, and with that first step taken towards the mountain-peaks of knowledge it is not too early to look forward to the day when they shall be received as men in the councils of their nation.

One thing that has struck me daily, as I have gone about the *bustees* to note progress and conditions, is the fine physique of these "untouchables," compared with higher-caste boys of their own age. Though small-built, they are lithe, active, and well-knit. One never sees among them those physical deformities of bad feeding and ill-health that are so common among the children of the very poor.

But, except for this superiority, I must confess that I find no marked difference of type. They seem to me to have, like other Hindus, the same faces that I have been accustomed to all my life, under slightly darker skins. If I had not known the country, I should have believed that this so-called Negritoid Pariah was as good an Aryan as myself; that he was no aboriginal, set to the hewing of wood and drawing of water for the race's sake, but one who had simply lost rank by that same process of trade-differentiation that certainly accounts for so many of the castes. These men are very dark, it is true—quite a chocolate-brown in some cases; but they are by no means uniformly so, and I have seen this particular colour sometimes in the highest classes, especially, as I fancy, where there is much exposure to the weather. Perhaps, however, there is greater irregularity of features amongst these pariahs than higher up in the social scale; but the question remains, whether this is due to race-inferiority, or to that freedom for individuality which must result from laxity of conventions. No one who has seen how the children of converted Jews lose the physiognomy of their forefathers will despise the influence of ideas on national types.

Anyway, whatever may be the future of our boys, for the present they are full of fun and enthusiasm. A really bad drain is quite a find to them all, and they work with patience and ardour, under supervision. For the real inferiority of the lower castes is that they require so much organisation and superintendence from their more fortunate countrymen. In the case of the one gang in which I am interested, three different people devote time and attention to overlooking the labour, and under these, again, there is the foreman of the gang; and every bit of this is absolutely necessary.

One of the most intolerable evils is the arrangement of bamboo "sanitary structures" in large clusters in the very centre and in close contact with dwelling-huts. These and the tanks—which continually receive sewage and other contaminations from the *bustees*—constitute the great permanent nuisances of the town. Nothing short of complete effacement could be efficient sanitation; but it should be added that the present state of things is of very long standing, and not an outgrowth of recent years.

In the pursuit of difficulties there is, I find, a limit at which toil becomes more or less sullen and despairing. Such toil for a scavenger can be found in one of the outlying districts of the Calcutta municipal area, where our workers discovered drains which would bid a fair defiance to Herakles himself. And there dwelt a Mussulman population, consisting of poultry, goats, and human beings in inextricable confusion.

There are open spaces with green grass in these villages, and visions of how it might be tantalise one as one explores—a well-flushed and repaired ditch; a pleasant village-green; a tree or a flowering shrub here and there. Given the land, these things ought not to be impossible for two thousand people paying municipal rates in one of the richest cities of the world. But we have had to keep twenty men digging for a week to get even a tiny stream of water to trickle feebly out of that terrible ditch. It had not been touched, they say, for fifteen years. And though we have swept the village-green, we have had no means for turning it into a garden, nor would we if we could, since we could not thereafter provide the wherewithal to keep it sweet and beautiful.

In the heart of this sordid quarter we come upon a little Moslem burying-ground. A low wall, pierced with a simple pattern, bounds it in restful curving lines. It is entirely without monuments or memorials, but in one corner a blasted tree of some sort—not unlike those grudging-leaved elders of the English Black Country—seems to stand for a landmark. And here, as they tell us, a holy man lies buried, and they, too poor to erect a stone, and too faithful to forget, have made shift with this old stump to keep green the memory of one who, poor like themselves, helped them years ago to live a fuller life.

A curious thing about a neighbourhood like this is that now and then one finds in it some old house and garden of great respectability. Is it a law of the growth of population that the poor inhabit always what the rich have left? How else can one explain the traces of past grandeur that one meets everywhere? In another *bustee*, surely one of the most hopeless of its sort, we find on the great central tank a ruined *ghât* that was once superb. The whole thing, with the reflection of the water in the sky, and the old tree that to this day bears its yearly load of glorious flame-coloured blossoms, is uncommonly like the picturesque and ruined villages of Kashmir.

One has to go down under the surface to see that the plague is here at all. When we hear in Europe that a place is "declared" stricken, we conjure up pictures of mortality in all its forms: grass growing on deserted pavements, houses marked with crosses, and the weird voice at midnight crying "Bring out your dead!" How different it really is! I first heard of the ravages of the disease at a European dinner party, and I came home and discovered that seven deaths had occurred in one week in my own lane.

Not a sound had betrayed the fact. The accustomed wailing had all been hushed. The dead had been buried or burned at night. Not one word to the outside world had betrayed the agony of the watchers by the beloved. Not one token told that men had dropped out of the ranks of the living. This was, of course, at the beginning of the outbreak. As time went on, the people realised, I think, that no outrage on their privacy was intended, and one began to meet the bearers more often about the streets, chanting *Rama Nama Satya hai* (The Name of the Lord alone is real) to their swinging pace, as they carried silent forms to the last rites; or one encountered one of those mournful Moslem processions by torchlight to the sound of the solemn *Allah illa, 'ill, 'ill Allah!* in the hour of dusk.

THE MEDIÆVAL UNIVERSITY OF INDIA

OF all the creations of a people—their art, their science, their customs, their building, and the like—the highest and most spiritual is their language. In this is expressed the soul of nations. In it is left the impress of their love and hope, their ideals of achievement and their criticism of the world.

Next to their country, there is no other single factor which does so much to determine the nature and destiny of a people as their own speech. Races and faiths come and go, children are born, grow old, and die. Each contributes as it can to the common tongue, but it remains superior to them all. As its language holds the soul of the nation, so in like fashion its literature holds the soul of the language. Each of the national factors wins recognition and immortality from the whole by its power to contribute ideas, characters, and forms of beauty to this, the dream-world of the race.

As one studies an Indian vernacular, the vastness and distinctiveness of the Indian dream-world continually grows on one. First there are the philosophical ideas which give its tone to the dream. Then there is the great gallery of ideal characters of which every Indian child by his birth is made a freeman, that gallery in which a man may wander all his life without one excursion into formal history: the dramatic background, as it were, of each generation of the national struggle. Then there are proverbs and fables innumerable, village-legends, quaint stories and metaphors, beggars' songs, ancestral hero-tales, cherished memories of saints and leaders, and all the floating literature that makes so large a part of the spiritual home of man without even incarnating itself in letters.

Gradually it dawns upon one that behind all this there is some central source of thought and strength, a fountain of authority, a standard of correctness that gives dignity and assurance. This academic authority lies in Sanskrit. Each of the Indian vernaculars throughout its long history has followed steadfastly in the wake of the classical tongue. All its higher literature has consisted of translations, and even where it has not been direct translation the *motif* has always claimed a Sanskrit source. In that language all the great culture of the nation has been preserved. Through it anyone might come in contact with the highest ideas of the race.

But Sanskrit is in itself a learned tongue; to acquire it takes many years of a man's life. The question arises: How has it been maintained in its purity and power from age to age? Each treasure is guarded and developed by its own social formation. What was the society, and what the education, that kept this living? Here we come upon the schools of the Brahmins. It is impossible to realise without some personal experience the definiteness and coherence of the old Hindu culture. Even to this day those who live near a family of ministering priests will hear father and son chanting the sacred texts, hour after hour, day after day, from morn onwards. To the Brahmin even his house is a school. But still more formal and absorbing was the organisation of the *tols* or schools of Sanskrit. With these India was netted from end to end, and men would come from the most distant parts to sit at the feet of some renowned teacher. The New Learning takes little note of university centres whose names are entered in no register, whose students are contented to work year after year for pure love of knowledge, without examination and without degree; where there is so little self-consciousness that no man ever thought of making a list of their names. Yet if disinterested love of truth and inheritance of deep and complex knowledge be the distinction of a university, the

New Learning with its great colleges and their immense revenues may well bow its head before the seats of learning of the Indian past. Benares and Nasik, Ujjain, Conjeeveram, and the ancient Taxila—to name only a few of the larger and more important of these seats—what pictures they call up to the mind's eye! Not all the provinces are famous for one thing. The South has kept the memory of the Vedas; Ujjain has held the palm in astronomy and mathematics, Benares in grammar, and Bengal in logic.

To any one of these, from the most distant parts of India, young students will travel, on foot for the most part, and beg, penniless, to be accepted by the chosen teacher. One in the days of Buddha desiring to learn medicine went all the way from Rajgir to Taxila, where Peshawar now stands. He was taken as a pupil by the great master of healing at whose door he knocked, and years passed happily by while he worked on, absorbed in the quest of knowledge. Then came the day when his master set him the final test, or as we should say, called for his doctor's thesis. He was to go out into the fields and bring in all the medicinal plants he knew. He went, but after long search he came back in great trouble of mind. He could not bring in all the healing herbs, he said, for all plants were of some use in medicine. And he demonstrated before his master the value to the physician of each one separately. Long afterwards, it is told, when he had returned as a great scholar to Magadha, this youth was allowed to heal Lord Buddha himself when he lay ill of a fever.

Such a glimpse of the ancient university remained as true in the days of Chaitanya of Nuddea, in the fifteenth century, as it was in the time from which it comes down to us. Nay, I have heard from an older generation how it was in their own boyhood, only the other day. It is a marvellously intense and earnest life that is revealed to us in the routine of the old *tols*. A household of some fifty or sixty students, distributed over a number of mud cottages arranged round a central tank, made up the college of a single teacher. They arrive at the age of twenty, perhaps, having broken the first ground of the subject of themselves, and would often remain unmarried till thirty-five. In at least one *tol* that I have heard of, at Vikramapore in Bengal, there were three students admitted from Maharashtra, for the fame of Bengal logic went far and wide, and all India knew the names of its best teachers. Here in such *tols* as this was lived out the great ideal of *brahmacharya*—the celibate student dwelling as a son in his master's house.

AN OLD COLLEGIATE VILLAGE

WE were a small and very cheerful party that set out to visit the village of Khardah. It was here that Nityananda—ordered by Chaitanya to take up the life of the householder—had dwelt year after year, organising and instructing the then rudimentary society of Vaishnavism. One day, about A.D. 1520, two thousand and five hundred men and women, "all Mussulmans," hearing of the great teacher of love and mercy, had come to him there to receive discipleship, and been admitted by him into Hinduism, as the order of *Nera-Neris*, or the Shaven-hes and the Shaven-shes. The records called them Mussulmans because to the writers they were not recognisable as Hindus, and it had been long ago forgotten that there could be any other category outside orthodox society to which they could belong. But they were in fact Buddhists, and that memorable day in the life of Nityananda definitely marked the death of Buddhism in Bengal.

Could a more fascinating question have been opened up? Within an hour or two we were on our way to examine what traces of such events were left in the place of their occurrence. The Ganges was full, and our little boat could not always keep us water-tight against the occasional downpour of rain that varied the monotony which uniformly fine weather would have caused. Near Baranagore began the long succession of temples and sacred spots that marked that part of the Ganges side which was always sacrosanct. As far as this, said someone, Chaitanya came, for is it not true that at Baranagore a house that Chaitanya visited still stands? From this point on we noticed every now and then a finer than ordinary bathing-*ghât*, distinguishing some old centre of importance; at Panihaty the evidences of a Moghul fort; again, the temple of the White Shiva, where in seasons of drought the peasants pray for rain, and so on. Still the question haunted us: would there at Khardah be any lingering sense of what the town had stood for in the past? Would the memory of Nityananda be alive in any real sense? Above all, could there possibly be any surviving tradition of the great event, of the incorporation of the *Nera-Neris* into Hinduism?

It seemed a wonderful story, this of Chaitanya and Nityananda, in the early sixteenth century. Surely there is no other country where the waking of genius is so welcomed as in India!

The love that was to spread to all mankind began to sweep Chaitanya of Nuddea into its whirlpools and torrents of ecstasy when he was eighteen only; and for three years more the foster-brother of his childhood shared with him every thought and enterprise. Then the inner call became imperious. Chaitanya could no longer brook the ways of the world, and saying farewell to all about him he wandered off, alone and free. But before he went, with strange prevision for one so planless of the work to be done for the world he was leaving, he begged Nityananda to enter the householder's life; and this behest was loyally carried out, his adopted brother living for the rest of his life here on the Ganges bank at Khardah. "And so," pursued the scholar, bent on expounding his own view, "it is really Nityananda to whom is due the formation of the Vaishnava community, and the working out of its rules for the admission of the lowly and the fallen into orthodox society. It was no fall from a higher life that led to the parting from Chaitanya. It was stern obedience and a sense of work to be done. This was that Nityananda who walked in the city without anger, without restlessness, and without pride. As for Chaitanya, he spent the next twenty-six years of his life, first in wandering, then at Brindaban, and then in the temple at Puri. He lived there for eighteen years, and there is not a village in Orissa where he is not worshipped. We of Bengal know him as a poor Brahmin. We have his pedigree, and can tell you of his family. But they in Orissa know him as God!"

In a deep quiet we came gradually to a fine old *ghât* made of tile-like bricks, with ornamental buildings at the top on each side. Near it stood a curious form of temple, made for the Exposition of the Image at the *Ras Mela*. And further in the town, though hidden from us here at the river bank, we knew that we should find the famous temple of Shyam Sundar, built by Nityananda himself.

It was the rainy season, most beautiful of all times for visiting the Ganges bank. The brimful river and the fresh green foliage gave an air of opulence and unusual beauty. But the great feature of the place one found as soon as landed to be the fine old buildings of the Gossain houses. Unplastered walls of brick displayed the exquisite work of the bricklayers, whose construction was of a quality to need no ornament. The houses in the quiet lanes of Khardah were like eighteenth-century colleges in some university city of the West: such was their air of perfect craftmanship and conscious dignity. We reminded ourselves, looking thus at the abodes of Nityananda's spiritual descendants, how probably the people living here had long forgotten the traditions of their home. Undoubtedly they must have shrunk by this time into the tightest shell of orthodoxy. One must not be too disappointed if they should prove the very reverse of what their ancestors would have had them. One could not expect that a great idea should persist, in its vigour, for four hundred years together in the same spot. Thinking thus, I came to the paved brick pathway that led to the temple of Shyam Sundar. Fascinated by the beauty o the paved way, I followed it and came to the precincts of the temple itself. As much as I could see from the entrance I saw, and after some moments was turning away, when an old Brahmin entered. "Oh no!" he cried; "come to this place in the *Nat-Mandir*. You can see better here." Considerably cheered by the warmth of the invitation, I followed his suggestion, while he went about his business in the temple. A few minutes later we found the place of the *Nera-Neris*. Sure enough, there it is to this day, kept in gracious memory by this very name, the lawn before the cottage-home of Nityananda, where the *Nera-Neris* were reabsorbed into their Mother-Church. The site of the house that once stood on the grass is now covered with an open veranda-floor, and the room in which Birbhadra, the son of Nityananda, was born is marked by a couple of *tulsi* plants. Here one can imagine Nityananda standing, in his doorway, when the whole twenty-five hundred camped before him to state their cases and accept his ruling. Beggar-men and women from all the countryside, they must have been only too conscious, many of them, that they were fallen and unworthy, in this way or that, and totally unaware of the great name they may once have borne. For many a generation, nay many a century, they had been constantly recruited by the failures of society, who shaved their heads and donned a copper-wire above the elbow, and with this mark of humility and religion, wearing the ochre-coloured cloth, sallied forth to beg their bread and impose on no one. Their name had long been held as a term of contempt, for were they not monks and nuns who wandered in pairs? Away with such mummery! said Bengal in effect. The crumbs from the richer tables were carelessly thrown to them, for the Indian people condemn none to starve, but their want of order and decency had made them a byword amongst men. Their very name was hurled carelessly at a new offender as a term of reproach. How strange that behind the courting of such a fate there is human suffering! The sinner continued to shave his head and adopt the garment of the order, and to sally forth with begging bowl in hand, and yet was keenly aware the while of the ignominy of his situation, would have given much, perhaps even complete self-reformation, to have met with a little respect from other human beings. Such was the sorry crowd that had camped on the lawn in those days at Khardah. Nay, as the villagers were presently telling us, even now there are *Nera-Neris*, and until lately it was the custom to give them a *mela* here once a year. Increasing poverty is making this impossible, and some of the older men among the local Gossains spoke of the fact in a broken-hearted fashion, as of an ancestral trust betrayed. But until a year or two ago the custom was maintained, and even now they are hoping to revive it. Nay, they were taking us presently to another temple—not of Shyam Sundar—built at a later date for the express purposes of the *mela*, and still used by the *Nera-Neris* as a *dharmsala*. This temple has never been finished, and consequently was never consecrated, but it is, curiously enough, built in the old-time fashion of Buddhist monasteries, as we see them at Mahavallipore; and this is fitting, since it has to afford sleeping quarters for so many who in name at least are of the religious.

The spirit of Nityananda, then, had not died out of Khardah. Nay, one can imagine the beggars—whose feet, in the European Middle Ages, some king was wont to wash with his own hands before sitting himself at the banqueting board—we can imagine these acquiring in the royal household a semi-symbolic character, as if within the palace beggars and kings were specially to be reverenced. And something of this spirit, I imagine, I detected at Khardah. The fact that we were strangers, and one of us a foreign woman, seemed to strike the good burghers as the very reason why we should be given civic entertainment, and presently we found ourselves once more on the way to the temple. They have heard the story of our tastes and predilections with attention and sympathy, and now they would show us something that would please us. They had a copy of *Bhagbat,* written by Nityananda with his own hand. Oh, that book! They held it before us and every word was a picture. Written with the old pens, on the old paper, with the old unfading ink, there was not a letter, not a space, not a word, that was not perfect. The very heart of Nityananda—free, sweet, rejoicing in beauty—seemed to be displayed before us. But what of the other relic? Of that one would speak, if one could, in whispers only. When Chaitanya commanded his brother to go back to the world, and take up there the life of householder and citizen, Nityananda broke his *sannyasin's* staff. And there is the head of it to this day in the temple at Khardah. They brought it out and held it up for us to see—the staff that was held in the hand of Nityananda, during those three wonderful years when he wandered side by side with Chaitanya through the villages and towns of Bengal, preaching love. We look in a dream at the simple broken piece of wood—only the head of the broken staff. But if we could see what you have seen, if we could touch what you have touched!

But Khardah does not retain merely the memory, or the relics, of its great happenings. It represents a community entrusted with a mission. For hundreds of years it has stood charged with the duty of teaching the inclusiveness of Hinduism. And were there not three strangers here, who on this account should be accorded the franchise of the place? Hence we could not depart from the temple till we had eaten *prasad*. All must gather together and eat it with us. Hurriedly it was sent for, and quickly consecrated, but already the twilight was falling when we tasted the communion, standing in the transept below the altar in the temple of Shyam Sundar. All Khardah, gentle and simple, Brahmin and lay folk, ate it with us; for all, it seems, come to make salutation at the evening *arati*. To one there it came with a sense of being "eaten in haste, with loins girt and staff in hand, for it was the Lord's Passover": and as, with many expressions of courtesy and respect, we turned away from the hurried feast, the bells rang out and the blaze of the light began for evening worship.

And so we dropped down the river in the starlight, thinking much of the making of history here in our close neighbourhood, and feeling all the wonder of a place that had not forgotten its mission in four hundred years.

THE HOLY CITY

THERE is a picture lately purchased by the committee of the Calcutta Art Gallery, which for those who know anything of the art of Mediæval Italy is full of significance.

Throughout the growth of the Mediterranean civilisations the student is constantly impressed by the vigour of the civic rather than the national ideal. We think clearly and continuously—not of Egypt, Judæa, Syria, Greece, Italy, Spain and Africa—but of Memphis, Thebes, Jerusalem, Tyre, Damascus, Ephesus, Athens, Rome, Carthage, and it may be a score or two of others. The state appears in our minds as merely a vague hinterlandlike appanage of the city thus conceived. Nor can we fail to see the influence which the pursuit of civic ideals has had upon the religious conceptions both of Judaism and of the Christianity which succeeds it.

It strikes upon an Indian ear as somewhat strange that the Jew should be able, in such good faith, to denote so much as he does simply by the use of the name of a municipality. "Send thee help from the sanctuary and strengthen thee out of Zion." We should find it difficult to say: "Send thee help from the sanctuary, and strengthen thee out of—Indraprastha," for instance. And yet why? But so deep was the habit of thought with the Jew that he has been able, through his incomparable literature, to stamp with a like vividness the names of many cities even outside Palestine proper, so that Babylon, Nineveh, and Damascus call up to this day certain larger than civic attributes which he, more or less justly, associated with them. It was natural enough, then, that a Judaic apostle should delineate Heaven as the New Jerusalem, that beloved city of his race. And it was in accordance with the ancestry of the Faith that the dreamers of the European Middle Ages should constantly present us with a Paradise that resembles a city or township much more closely than a country or a fatherland. Even Dante and Giotto, in spite of the enormous grasp of their minds, were both civic dreamers, and it seemed natural to them that Beatrice should shine as fair in Heaven as she shone in Florence.

The cursory reader might regard it as a foregone conclusion that such civic passion as this was never known in India. For even Benares—which resembles Jerusalem in being a sacred city of no less than three religions—even Benares is more strictly national than civic in its character. Every state in India had built a palace within the sacred area. Every religion possesses there a cathedral, and its charities from the municipal point of view are apt to fail. Colleges of Sanskrit learning, almonries of daily doles for pilgrims and poor students; monasteries filled with devotees—all these do not suffice for the needs of the city from that purely territorial point of view which is the civic spirit proper, and the evolution of charities having this aim has been left for modern times. And yet, there have in all ages been great and resonant names in India that should give us pause ere we venture to arrive at the sweeping conclusion that civic passion is foreign to the Indian spirit. What about Chitore, that rock-built crown of the Rajput deserts? What about Delhi, Amritsar, Poona, Conjeeveram, and a hundred others? Yes, and one more, one which stands revealed in this picture newly brought to Calcutta —what about Ayodhya?

It is a small picture, measuring not many inches either way. The colours are rich and mellow, in the old missal-like style of Indian painting. The foreground is filled with a scarf-like band of figures, painted for the most part in ginger-shades of orange and yellow. Behind riset he white marble walls and towers of Ayodhya, and beyond only a narrow strip of sky is seen above the horizon.

To those familiar with the Madonna and Child of Italian painters the figures in the front are easy to understand. Under the umbrella of state—which, by the way, is decorated with real pearls, and suggests the *baldachino* of Roman churches—sit Sita and Rama on a double throne. In Rama's hand is an exquisitely decorative white lotus, reminiscent of the Annunciation lily of the angelic messenger. On the right of the king stand his brothers, on the left of the queen her ladies of honour, and Hanuman kneels at the feet of the royal pair. The scene is laid in the gardens of Ayodhya. In the moat behind, bathers and a couple of elephants are seen, swimming and sporting in the water, and the royal barge is shown in all its glory.

But it is on the snow-white buildings of Ayodhya that stretch from beyond the moat into the blue that the artist has spent all his powers. Intending perhaps to delineate a palace, he has actually given us a city, filled with life and motion and happiness. But it is the city of Paradise. No human scene, alas, was ever poised so dream-like between earth and heaven. No human scene was ever so perfect, growing more and more distinct as we examine it closer and in greater detail.

CHITORE

It was almost midnight, as the moon grew near the full, when we looked for the first time on the fortress of Chitore. The lights in the village at its foot had been extinguished, and the hill with its great length stood dark and isolated against the sky. Almost directly above the black cleft of the Cow's Mouth stood the Tower of Victory of Kumbha Rana, like a finger pointing upwards in witness of past glory. And even in the darkness we could see the gentle curving lines of the walls following the contour of hillside, with its three miles of length and one of breadth. Silently we sat on a low stone a mile off and drank in the scene. Even thus, on the first or last night of his journey, may some Rajput of old have gazed hour after hour on this beloved home. Even thus may Padmini have caught her first glimpse of this city of her fate!

It is not a connected story, this for which Chitore is famous. The wild romance of which her annals are so full is a series of gleams and flashes, lasting through hundreds of years. Like watching from the plain the escalade of some rocky summit is the effort of one who strives to picture the past of Chitore. Again and again do the banners of the clansmen appear amidst trees and crags, only again and again to be lost to sight. Wherever the mists of history lift, there are revealed the old-time ideals of the courage and pride of woman and the glory of man. Chitore is no mere chronological record ; she is an eternal symbol, the heart's heart of one phase of the Indian genius.

Architecturally the splendour of the city justifies her pride. The rock on which she stands slopes inwards from all sides, with the result that there are innumerable tanks and a water supply practically unlimited. Within the walls are the remains of what has been virtually two cities, one to the north-east, the ancient capital of the time before Bappa Raoul, and one more modern which grew up between his accession in A.D. 728 and the evacuation under Akbar in 1568.

The old manor-grange, on whose veranda Bappa Raoul, in the eighth century, administered justice, scarcely comports with our modern notions of a palace. In front of it, not far away, is a Tower of Victory, now crumbling to pieces, and everywhere the living rock of the original foundation is close at hand. The life of the garrison within this fortress must have been strangely like that of a camp.

Long and narrow, like some lean grey lion crouching for the spring, lies walled Chitore on its craggy hill. And the newly-arrived traveller watching it may see it to-night, as the returning escort may have seen it when Padmini's marriage procession halted for the last time on the homeward way, more than seven centuries ago. Then, as now, the long heavy walls curved lovingly, like the canvas of a tent, about the city. Little can the "lotus fair" Padmini have slept that night, the last of the long journey from her father's distant stronghold. Rather must she have gazed on through hour after hour of waking dreamfulness, counting the tale of the turrets and bastions of the fortress that to-morrow she would enter as bride and queen. Within her was the confidence of the Indian wife, who thinks of herself as beginning what is only a new chapter in an old story, as recovering a thread that was held but a while ago, and dropped at death. Not for the first time were they to take up to-morrow the tale of life together—it was an ancient comradeship of the soul. Did no vision of the future cast its shadow across the path before her to make Padmini shrink and pause, in the glory of this her great homecoming? Had the bard whispered no word above her cradle of the tragedy of greatness that lay before her? Did she know that as long as winds should wail over Chitore they would sing her name, that with her would every stone and every building be associated in the world's memory till the end of time? To her, what would be was but the following of the path of Rajput honour. Was it not always said that, in the hour of birth, the eyes of a boy were set upon a knife and those of a girl upon a lamp—for the man must leave life by way of the sword and woman by that of fire?

AN INDIAN AMULET

It lies beside me as I write, a heavy heart-shaped ornament, in pale old bronze. On it, in low relief, is a quaint design of peacocks, pecking their mutual beaks into a conventional-looking pot of basil that stands between them. Its worth, in money, is some few farthings. For little more it was bought; sold, doubtless, for something less; and it is worn only by such as can at no time in their frugal lives afford the few shillings necessary to buy its like in silver.

And yet, poor as it is, this Indian amulet may have been an heirloom in its time. Generation after generation of mothers may have worn it daily, as they went forth at dawn, and came back at sunset; worn it alike at toil and at rest. Time after time may it have been handed on to the little daughter on her marriage, or to the daughter-in-law when welcomed for the first time to the peasant-home. Or the chain, or string of coins, on which it hung, has been unclasped for ever maybe by the wearer in the bitter hours of widowhood, or reverently lifted by a sorrowful son or daughter ere the dead form of the mother was borne forth to the village burning-ghât. For it belongs, this simple rustic ornament, to another order than the present. It comes of the time when no hard-and-fast line divided art from industry; when, every need being met by manual toil, the enthusiasm of the creator limited his work, and possessions could not be quickly changed but must be made strong to accumulate from age to age. The farmhouse kitchen of a century ago in Europe, shining with oak and brass; the border of the Kashmir shawl in India, transferred by skilful fingers from one web to another; and this amulet of mine, are not modern in kind and origin, but mediæval.

If only it could utter all the secrets it may remember, what might we not hope to hear! For according to the customs of Silâo, whence it came, the place of this amulet is over the heart of the village maid. Thus it has lain year in year out; and of the things that tell themselves in silence, by the catching of a breath or the quickening of a pulse; of the long sweet tale of wifely happiness and motherly cares; of the struggle with poverty and the achievement of prosperity; of moments of rapture and insight, kneeling before some image in a temple, or watching the cows wend home at time of cowdust—of all these things how much it has heard! How much, could it but speak, it might reveal!

And yet the story, told in such fashion and from such a viewpoint, might after all seem strangely familiar. For it is open to question whether there be much distance between the humanity of any two villages, though one be Indian and the other English or Italian. In externals, of course, their characteristics are strongly marked—there is no mistaking one for another. I cannot forget the first time I saw that ancient market-town in Behar, which is known as Silâo. How interesting a province is Behar itself! The traveller in Brittany has heard the peasants talk of "going into France," and similarly in Behar, though it is an integral part of Bengal, one drops instinctively into the Breton attitude, and thinks of the Gangetic Plain as of a foreign country. And Silâo is really ancient, in the Eastern sense. It is only a tiny township, built of mud, yet it is quite possible that its popped rice was as famous in the countryside thirty-five centuries ago as it is to-day. So long since, at least, was probably the first appearance of the neighbourhood on the stage of history. The very dust is fraught with memories. On the time-worn highroad, between Baragaon, the old university of Nalanda, and Rajgir, the pre-Asokan capital of the kings of Bengal, stands the village, in the midst of the far-stretching green of its fields of rice. And through it Buddha must have passed, ere he overtook the great multitude of goats going up to the sacrifice, and, according to the legend, lifted the lame kid and carried it on his neck, that it might keep pace with the herds. Often and often, even now, one may meet with such good shepherds on the roads about Silâo, and still better, a few miles farther on, outside the modern village of Rajgir. Daily there, from dawn almost till noon, the constant patter of hoofs large and small betokens the passing of hundreds of cows, buffaloes, sheep, and goats out of the village, through the mountain-defile, with its hot springs, into the pastures that cover to-day the hillsides and the ruins of Old Rajgir. And here again, as afternoon draws on to dusk, one may witness the return homeward of the flocks, or, later, watch while a missing cow or two comes crashing through the brushwood, in answer to the call of the herdsman from the out-standing rocks by the stream-side. It is then that one may be happy enough to meet a belated goat-herd, his form looming larger than common through the quickly-passing twilight, who could not but have lingered, because, while he bears some foot-sore little one, he also leads perhaps a weary mother, tenderly, along the darkening road.

There are women-tenders of the herds, as well as men. Tall they are, and free of gait, very gentle, and very very proud, these Hindu women of the old rustic world. Their costumes alone would be sufficient to mark them out as beautiful and distinguished, though they are mere peasant folk; for it is rarely that one meets here even a widow wearing the stainless white of the higher classes of Bengal. Crimson and green and scarlet are, in Behar, the favourite colours for the *sari*—that long broad scarf, which forms the main garment as well as the veil of the Indian woman. The coarse clinging cotton, covering the head and falling thence to the waist to form the skirt, is embroidered all over, in a bold effective stitch, with the little curling pine-cone, or palmetto, that is so characteristic an element in Indian decoration. Long long ago these women have forgotten its why and wherefore. They would not dream of connecting their adoption of the admired design with the emblematic jewel on a royal turban; and yet it is not unlikely that their constant use of the pattern perpetuates the fact that six hundred years, or perhaps a thousand, before Christ, Rajgir was a King's burgh.

Quite as beautiful as the *sari*, in its own way, is the little bodice—oftenest of dark blue, outlined with scarlet—that covers the bust and falls severely from the throat to conceal the head of the skirt. It is cut back at the neck leaving the head free, and the tight sleeves go only half-way to the elbow. Its greatest beauty, however, lies in its straightness: there is very little cutting-out in ancient costume. In the Greek *chiton,* the Japanese *kimono,* the Himalayan *choga,* and in this *jama* and *sari* of Northern India there is too much respect for the lines of material to suffer the figure-modelling that we call dress-making. So this Behari blouse or *jama* is made only of four pieces—two breadths back and front and a half-breadth added under each arm, as *modistes* might say—and they are all straight. But oh, how lissom and willowy is the figure within! And how commandingly beautiful is often the dark face, with its large brown eyes shadowed by the rich colours of the veil!

It was our first visit to Silâo, and we were in the very middle of the bazaar, where three roads meet. We had clattered in our noisy vehicles up the village street; past the old brass-shop, where an Indian girl-friend, who had come like myself from the city, would one day find and bring to me my amulet; past the village school, where twelve or fifteen tousle-headed urchins were learning the three R's with the mud floor for writing-surface; past the confectioners' shops, with the fishes and peacocks cut in brass swinging in a row along the front for sign-boards. We had reached the very thickest part of the modest traffic, and had swung recklessly round the corner to the right, when, a few paces down the street we were leaving on one side, we caught sight of a girl standing—tall, starry-eyed, and queenly. Her age may have been eighteen or twenty. She was dressed in green, and stood there—sky and temple in the background—with the frank look of a child, entirely unconscious of observation. But her arms held the long stems, while the white buds slept against each shoulder, of two great sheaves of water-lilies.

So buying and selling and eating and clothing are not the whole life of Silâo. It was another proof, could one have been so foolish as to need more, that no poet from the city can ever gaze so deep as the farm and forest folk themselves into the beauty of Nature. For these blossoms had been gathered but an hour before, from the ponds among the rice-fields. They are the commonest wild things of that peasant world, where they are known as "the lovers of the moon," because they open at nightfall—unlike the lordly lotus, who watches open-eyed the footsteps of the sun. And here they were offered for sale by one who had looked into their golden hearts and known their loveliness, to any who might be fain to lay flowers and prayers at the feet of God in the temple beyond. The green-clad woman with her lilies stood in the busy market-place, as the silent incarnation of the call to morning worship.

O sane and simple life of the Indian villages, firm-poised betwixt the Unseen and the Seen! is it of this my amulet would speak to me? Coming from some other peasant woman, in all likelihood dead and gone, is the message that her lips too would utter through it if they could, this same, of priest and chant and worshipper, and of some tiny tabernacle, shadowed and lily-strewn and cool, that stands in an Indian village as the place of morning-prayer?

KING PARIKSHIT AND THE FROG MAIDEN

ONCE upon a time there reigned over the city of Ayodhya a king of royal race, named Parikshit. And Parikshit on a certain day, being out hunting and pursuing a deer, outstripped all his companions and wandered alone in a dense dark forest, far away from human habitations. Now the king was both weary and a-hungered, and seeing the cool shadows, and catching sight of a beautiful pool, he pushed forward and plunged in, with the idea of bathing and resting. And when both he and his horse were cool and refreshed, he gathered lotus leaves and stems and placed them before the animal, and he himself lay down on the short grass beneath the trees.

As he lay there, between sleeping and waking, he heard the sound of a sweet voice singing. In his astonishment he sat up, to see who could be in his neighbourhood, for nowhere had he seen the footprints of men, nor had he supposed that he was near human dwellings. As he watched he saw, through the bushes, a maiden gathering flowers, and she was of a surpassing loveliness and sang as she plucked. Presently, in her quest of flowers, she drew unwittingly near the king, and he held his breath with sheer delight at the beauty of her voice and features.

At last he resolved to speak. "Blessed one," he said gently, "who art thou? and whose?"

"Whose?" said the girl, with a start, "I? I belong to none. I am unwed."

"Unwed?" said the king, "oh do then, I pray thee, grant thyself to me!"

"If I did," said the maiden slowly and pensively, "If I did, I should require a promise—!"

"What promise couldst thou ask," cried the enamoured king, "that I could not grant? Speak! What is it?"

"If I am to marry thee," said the damsel mysteriously, "thou must give me a pledge that never wouldst thou ask me to look upon water. Unless I had this promise, I could not wed." And as she spoke she cast upon the king a look of such more than mortal sweetness that he felt as if he would swoon away.

"Dear heart," cried Parikshit, "what a little thing were this to stand between us! From the moment that thou art mine, I promise thee never to ask thee to cast thine eyes on water."

And the maiden, hearing this, bowed her head, and they exchanged tokens of marriage, and hand in hand sat down on the grass together in silence. And as they remained thus, the king's friends and escort came up, having searched for and followed him. And finding him thus in the company of a newly-affianced bride, a state carriage was brought, and the two entered it, and were driven back to the capital together.

Now from this time forward, it was as if some strange enchantment had been woven about the king. He was always in the private apartments with his newly-wedded queen. And instead of his absorption in her growing less, it seemed to become stronger and stronger, till none could obtain access to him, and the royal ministers were refused audience.

When this was on the verge of becoming a public scandal, the chief minister sent for one of the waiting-women about the palace, and questioned her closely concerning the nature of her who had so infatuated their sovereign. And the maid said: "Her beauty is undeniable and unsurpassed. In charm and loveliness she is without a peer. But one thing about her is very strange. The king was able to marry her only after promising that he would never show her water."

Now when the prime minister heard this he went away and caused a royal park to be laid out, well-planted with trees that were laden with flowers and fruit. And in a hidden place within the park he dug a beautiful bathing-pool, filled with water that was sweet as nectar, and well covered with a net of pearls. And when it was finished he came privately one day to the monarch and said, "Here is a delightful forest without water. Let it be used for the royal pleasure." And, hearing this, the king and his adored queen went out into the park and wandered about its lawns and glades. And at last, being tired and spent, and not altogether free from hunger and thirst, the king caught sight of a charming bower, all festooned with the white and fragrant bells of creeping plants.

"Come, beloved!" he said to the queen, "here is an arbour that was made for rest. Let us enter." And they entered.

But when he was within, the king saw that the bower only covered the bathing-stairs of a bathing pool, which was shaded by some sort of roof that looked like cobweb, and being unspeakably attracted by all the surroundings and the sparkling coolness of the waters, he turned to his wife and said gently, "Surely no harm would happen to you if you bathed here! Would you not like to do so?"

Scarcely were the words uttered than the queen stepped merrily to the water-side and took a plunge. The waters closed over her as she dived, and Parikshit waited, half doubtfully, for her return. Alas, it was in vain. She did not reappear. The wife he adored was lost to him, it seemed, for ever.

Mad with anxiety, the king ran hither and thither, searching for his beloved. Nowhere could he recover any trace of her. He had the lake dragged, but even her body was not to be found. Then he ordered that the waters should be baled out. But when this had been done, nothing was discovered, save a large frog sitting beside a hole.

At this sight the king leapt to the conclusion that his wife had been devoured by frogs, and his wrath against the whole race was without bounds. Wherefore he promulgated an order that throughout his dominions they were to be slain, and that no one was to appear before him without a tribute of dead frogs.

Soon in the world of frogs this state of things became evident. Not one of them could appear above ground without the fear of instant death. And the whole tribe was afflicted with unspeakable terror. In their extremity they went in embassy, with the story of their wrongs, to their own king, and he in the guise of a begging friar appeared before the throne of Parikshit, and urged him in the name of religious gentleness and mercy to rescind his cruel order for the destruction of the poor frogs. But Parikshit, with his whole soul filled with woe for the death of her who was so dear to him, replied only with renewed protestations of anger and revenge. Had the frogs, he said, not swallowed up one who was to him as the heart of his heart? Why then should he ever forgive them? Rather than do so he would continue to slay them with a continually renewed fury. It was surely very far from fitting that a learned man should intercede on their behalf.

As the monarch spoke of the loss he had suffered the seeming beggar before him looked pained and startled. It was clear that he suddenly understood the situation. "Alas, alas!" he said, "thou art under a fascination, O king! Look upon me. I am Ayu, the king of the frogs, and she who was thy wife is my daughter Susobhana. She has cast a glamour over thee, who art of the race of men and not of our kindred. She hath indeed the power to cast enchantments. By this her conduct I am deeply grieved!"

But when Parikshit heard that he had before him the father of his beloved he said only, "Oh sir, if she is thy daughter, then bestow her upon me! I desire nothing save her return."

Then the king of the frogs, standing before Parikshit, summoned his daughter, and when she appeared before him he joined her hand to that of the monarch, saying, "Serve and wait upon thy lord!" And Parikshit, feeling out of his great love for his wife that in her restoration he had obtained as it were the sovereignty of the three worlds, bowed down before the king of the frogs, and did him reverence in due form, as the father of his beloved, and with voice choked by joy and tears, said, "Oh how fortunate I am! How fortunate I am!" And the King of the Frogs, taking leave of his daughter, left them, and returned to that place from which he had come.

Now the King of the Frogs had parted from his daughter in sorrow and grave disapproval of the spell originally cast by her, whereby the innocent king and all her own people suffered so deeply; and in the moment of farewell, as is the wont of fathers, he had looked into the future, and instead of blessing her, had sternly said, "The fruit of the enchantment that thou so wrongfully hast practised will be seen as a flaw in the kingly honour of thy children, until the magic spell shall be redeemed." This, then, was the doom that hung over the dynasty of Parikshit and the frog-maiden, till it should be redeemed. And they lived happily together, and had three sons, whose names were Sala, Dala, and Vala. And in fulness of time King Parikshit gave up the world, and, placing his eldest son upon his throne, himself retired into the forest.

Now it happened that Sala, the new king, while out hunting one day, saw a very fleet deer, and urged his charioteer to drive quickly that he might catch it.

But the charioteer answered, "It is impossible. Only a pair of Vami horses could have enabled us to overtake that deer!" Now these Vami horses of which he spoke belonged to Vamadevá, a great Brahmin scholar, who lived in the ashrama beside the Ganges.

And when the king heard of them he became possessed of a desire to be driven by them, and, going to the ashrama of Vamadeva, he begged that he would lend them to him that he might capture a fleet deer. And the holy man consented to the king's using them, but exacted a promise that they should be returned immediately. Alas, the Vami horses proved so excellent that the king coveted them, and forgot his promise, but kept them when his business of hunting was over and locked them up in secret stables attached to his palace!

Now when Vamadeva saw that his horses were not returned he became very sorrowful, for he felt that the king's plighted word could not be trusted. After waiting for a month, he sent a disciple to the sovereign to receive from him the Vami steeds. But the king told the young man that these horses were fit only for the use of kings, and that he could not understand why holy men and scholars should expect to possess them.

So the disciple had to return to his master without the horses.

Then Vamadeva himself appeared before the monarch and pleaded with him to render back his property, which he had promised, moreover, to return when his need should be over.

But the king was obdurate, being unable, by reason of the blemish on his birth, to perceive in their fulness the obligations of the royal honour. He offered the rishi anything out of his own stables that he might choose to take; he undertook to appoint Vamadeva the chief priest of the kingdom; he promised anything and everything, only he would not give back to their rightful owner the horses he coveted.

Then Vamadeva called upon four terrible demons to appear and slay the impious king, and even as he was speaking they arose suddenly, armed with lances, and, advancing from the four quarters, felled him to the earth. Thus died Sala the king, and Dala his brother reigned in his stead.

Now as soon as there was a convenient time, Vamadeva came before the new king and asked that the pair of Vami horses now in the royal stables should be bestowed upon him. But Dala, instead of answering, turned to his charioteer and ordered him to bring one of his finest arrows, tempered with poison, that he might kill Vamadeva. But when he raised his arm to point the arrow the Brahmin said quietly, "Thou are not aiming at me, O king! Rather is thine arrow pointed against thine own son, Senajit; him art thou about to slay."

As the words were spoken the king let fly his terrible arrow, and at the selfsame moment, in the innermost apartments of the palace, the child Senajit fell, pierced by the arrow from his father's hand.

Suddenly the wail of mourning was heard, and a panic-stricken messenger arrived to give the king the news of the disaster to his line. But the death of his son seemed only to drive Dala to a frenzy of anger. Demanding another arrow, he called upon gods and men, his own subjects and the denizens of the heaven, to be witnesses of the death he was about to deal; and again he raised his arm to take the fatal aim. . . .

To the amazement of all present, except the Brahmin, who stood as he was, with eyes fixed on the sovereign, without moving—the bow was not twanged, nor was the arrow shot forth. A look of agony passed over the king's face; his hands shook, and he stood still. At last with a groan he said, "I am defeated. I am overcome. I am unable to bring about the death of Vamadeva!" And his right hand fell nerveless to his side.

At this Vamadeva's aspect became all gentleness and kindness. "Send for thy queen, O king!"

said he, "and let her touch this arrow that thou didst destine for murder. Thus mayst thou be purified from the fruit of thy sin."

And the king did as he was bidden, sending for his queen. And when she came she did reverence to the sage Vamadeva, and stretched out her hand to take the poisoned arrow. And the holy man was much touched by the nobility of her bearing and the grace of her salutation, and blessing her, he said, "O thou that art without fault, ask thou of me an incomparable boon. It is mine to grant thee whatever thou shalt ask!"

And the queen answered, "I pray that my husband may be freed from his sin, and that I may be ever his helpmeet, to aid him in the growth of happiness and virtue."

"O good as thou art beautiful!" cried the delighted rishi, "thou hast saved this royal house! With thee is the curse departed that was spoken by Ayu, the father of Susobhana. What woman doomed, a woman hath redeemed. Rule thou, O princess, over the hearts of these thy kinsmen, thy husband and thy son, and over this great kingdom of Ayodhya. Never, while they honour thee, shall there be loss of kingly honour in the race of Parikshit!"

And so saying, and taking back his horses, the rishi departed from the court of Dala, the king of Ayodhya.

GOPALER-MA: THE MOTHER OF THE CHRIST-CHILD

INDIAN languages are curiously rich in tender diminutives, the use of which so much depends on association that they are incapable of translation. It is clear, for instance, that if we address a little girl of three as *Ma*, or a boy of the same age as *Bap*, that delicate mingling of gravity and laughter which we intend to convey is a matter entirely of the colour of the voice, and will defy any attempt to render it in a foreign tongue. One of the most striking words of this class is *Gopala*. Literally, it means the Cowherd, referring to Krishna—the Krishna of Brindaban. But it has been so appropriated in this regard that its actual significance can only be rendered in English as "Christ-Child," and the woman who folds her baby-boy closer, calling him Gopala, is paralleled amongst English mothers only by one who thinks of her child as the Christ-Child, come to her out of night and storm seeking to find His Own. In this sense the name is often on the lips of all our household. For in one of the rooms of our zenana lives an old

old woman, who is known as *Gopaler-Ma*, the Christ-Child's Mother.

. . . .

All night long we had been watching the slow hard breathing of the dying. In, in, in, it would go, growing ever more and more still, till one thought that never again could any movement occur in the aged frame, and then freedom once more and a succession of quick deep inbreathings. Such breathing, they said, was seen but seldom, and was the result of long years of *Pranayama*, practised unconsciously over the beads, as night and day the old woman had counted them, saying the name of her *Ishtam*, "Gopala, Gopala, Gopala!"

For she beside whom we sat and watched was Gopaler-Ma, that saint whom Sri Ramakrishna himself had treated as his mother.

Without a single want she lay there, as she had lived, the mind suspended in the thought that had made its life, the face full of the last sweetness and peace. A day and a night already had she lain thus by the Ganges side. For at the moment of the rising of the full moon, we had stepped with her over the threshold of the door, and had felt the silent soaring of her spirit, as it cast off triumphantly the first of its outer wrappings, the shell of home. But when she had reached the *ghâts*, and lain awhile in the play of cool breezes and the brightness of the moon, she had shown, as the dying are wont to do, some signs of revival. And the candle of life for many an hour thereafter had burnt up in its worn socket, before it was finally to be put out.

It was not, perhaps, entire unconsciousness in which she lay. For to one and another it would seem, now and again, as if she gave a look of recognition, following them with her eyes. And on that last morning, when a Brahmin came and chanted above her *slokas* from the Upanishads, she had responded visibly, with what would almost represent excitement. All her life long she had worshipped the idea of the Holy Child, and now there seemed a fitness in the fact that at the last, dying of old age at over ninety years, the worn-out frame had gone back to babyhood again, and the twitching of the limbs or the turning of the head was the only sign of volition she could give.

But even this had been sometime past, for now that night was with us once again, she had lain still for many hours, with all the consciousness turned inward, and the peace of one who asked nothing of the world about her.

We, the waiting women, could hear from without the long low lapping of the Ganges against the foot of the bathing-stairs, and the moaning whisper of the rain-winds as now and again they swept down and caught the surface of the waters. And once, was it at midnight, or was it an hour or so later?—once in the midst of the silence there came a rushing and swirling of the river beneath the cloud-veiled moon, and the little boats lying at anchor on the Ganges knocked against each other, and the word went round, "The tide is coming in!" But some, to whom the passing soul had been friend and *Guru*, sighed, for with the turn of that tide had we not been warned that she would go forth, and her place and people know her no more?

Hour upon hour had gone and still no change. Some who had rested rose, and plied little offices of tenderness beside the sick, and another lay down to snatch a spell of sleep. Suddenly there was a stir, and a light hand touched the sleeper. "Call the bearers," said one, "for the end is come!" Out on the terrace above the river-steps they sat, as they had sat all night, holding deep talk of the past, and of the Lives with which this life outgoing here had been a link, and easy enough were they to call. A moment more and the dying form was lifted to the cot, and then, on the shoulders of yellow and white clad bearers together, it was borne swiftly out of the room to the north, and then down the few steps that it needed to take Gopaler-Ma where she could lie with feet touching the sacred waters, and so go forth.

There she lay, the last changed breaths coming at easy intervals, while one of the monks, whom she had known as boys, bent over her and with his brow to hers, half spoke, half whispered the words that the Hindu loves to hear in his last hour—*Om Ganga Narayana! Om Ganga Narayana Brahma!* A moment more, and then with one voice from the circle of watchers came the shou tof *Haribol!* for the last breath had gone. The spirit of Gopaler-Ma had taken flight, and only the garment of flesh was left behind.

Then one at the head of the bier, looking up at the brightening of the sky behind the clouds asked, "Is this the dawn?" And from the foot came back the answer, "Yes it is the dawn!" And then, looking down, we saw that the waters that had bathed the feet of the dying were already receding—were already sunken some inches below us. Gopaler-Ma had died indeed at the moment of dawn, on the very turn of the outgoing tide.

THE INDIAN ASH, OR TREE OF HEALING

HOW full of a mystic antiquity are the names of the lotus, the olive, and the ash! Ancient Egypt, Greece, and Scandinavia spring to our minds as the words are heard. The syllables seem haunted to this day by the dryads that the Greek mind saw in every tree. They carry us back to the age of the nymphs who made their home in pools and seas. There was a time when nature seemed to man but as the garment of some large sweet presence that lived and breathed within it. Alas, that age is gone. Irish elder and quicken still point to the neighbourhood of the Neolithic doorsill, but no longer are they held to guard the village with their mysterious benedictions. The olive yields, as of old, the sacred berries and the oil, but Athene has fled from the hearts where she made her home. Only in India the ancient thought lives on. Here, still, the women hush their voices and bow their heads as they pass before the tree of healing called the *neem*. Here, still, the earth at its foot forms a rude altar, and a protruding fragment of pointed stone, unchiselled, stands as the symbol of that great mother of all, whose golden-green home is the sunny spot beneath the boughs.

If we take as our standard, not the rigid classifications that appeal to the botanist, but those visible affinities that stir popular recognition, we shall probably feel that the *neem*—with its fern-like leaves, its feathery branches of small golden-green fruits, its wide-spreading roots, and gnarled and slender growth—is but the tropical equivalent for the ash of Northern Europe, or the olive of the Mediterranean. Some of us may have been puzzled to account for the prominence of the ash in Celtic, and still more in Norse, mythology. Why should the Scandinavian Yggdrasil, tree of eternity, have been an ash, with its roots in the past, its stem in the present, and its crown of leafage in the future? Why should the first man, Askr, have been born of it? The ash is not so plentiful as to account for this. It forms no forests in the lands where it is sacred, like the beech or oak. Just as we know that the men who taught to their children the dream of Asgard had come to the north along the old trade-routes from the beautiful cities of Asia, Nineveh, and Babylon, with all their wealth, luxury, and refinement, so also we cannot resist the conclusion that the ash derived its importance from their recognition of it as a tree with which, elsewhere, they had been familiar. This argument cannot, of course, be complete until some intermediate tree is discovered in Persia, and its folk-lore noted and studied. For the ash was especially associated in Europe with the Age of Bronze, bringing in the horse and his sacrifice, and the key to this as a state ceremonial can only be sought in Mesopotamia—with the crossings of the highways that made Nineveh and Babylon—and in neighbouring districts of Persia and Asia Minor. If Mohammedanism in those countries is anything like what it is in India, or if its action has been at all like that of Buddhism in the farther East, it must have preserved a great deal amongst the lower orders of society that could never claim recognition from the higher; and much still remains to be discovered regarding the connection between the worship of the sun, to whom the horse was always sacrificed, and some particular sacred tree. A trace of this connection lingers still amongst the Kayasths of Bengal, who will not gather the leaves or twigs of the *neem* on Sunday, because it and the cow, they say, had their birth on the sun's day; and there are people who, though they worship the great Mother, do not associate her presence particularly with the *neem* except in her specialised form of Sitola Devi.

Wonderful properties of nourishment and healing belong to this, the Indian ash. Its leaves are used for medicine and for food. A man may actually live on a handful of them eaten daily, and with milk they make an abundant and satisfying diet. The acrid berries, like tiny olives, provide lamp-oil and unguents for the very poor. Even the winds that blow through it are laden with soothing and with health, so that an old custom in Calcutta plants a *neem* tree on the east of the house, that the fever-breeze may be robbed of its poison ere it reaches the homestead and touches the beloved. And on both sides of the old Mahratta Ditch that once enclosed the city, the Circular Road as it is now, we may still trace an old avenue of *neem* trees—for is not the city the home of its children? And last of all, when the tree of healing grows old there sometimes breaks from its heart, it is said, the silver-white stream of the *neem* milk. This gushes out, intermittently, for months together, and people flock from all over the countryside to see the sight. Every drop of the precious fluid is gathered up and preserved for the healing of disease, and whole generations after talk of the miraculous spring.

Out of the very night of time, from long before the dawn of history, come some of these most familiar associations of the Indian folk. There are two or three sacred trees, all of them undoubtedly very ancient. Low-caste Mohammedan women make offerings to the spirit of healing that dwells in the *bo*, or *aswattha*, the sacred tree of Buddhist times. This may be a remnant of long pre-Buddhist worship, or it may be only another exemplification of the universal law that Islam in India followed directly in the footsteps of Buddhism. In Orissa again, and Chota Nagpur, and some districts north of Benares, a like worship is paid by certain strictly aboriginal castes to the *palash* tree—*Butea frondosa*—with its scarlet plume-like flowers, borne on naked boughs. Under this tree, it is said, there used to be offered the dread agricultural rite of human sacrifice to Miri-Amma, the Earth-Mother. It gave its name, again, to the people who dwelt, in the days of Buddha, to the east of Pataliputra, against whom Ajatasatru built the fortress that was afterwards to become the seat of empire. The castes that still pay reverence to the *palash*, associating with it the name of Miri, represent doubtless this ancient people, the Palasii of Megasthenes.

Still vaster is the antiquity that stands revealed in the universal association of these trees with feminine divinities. It is true enough, as some have maintained, that the drama of nature is the subject-matter of all mythology, and that therefore, by tracing out the unity of myths, we ought to be able to disentangle the great primitive spectacle fundamental to all. But into his interpretation of this drama man could not fail to import conceptions derived from the social forms about him and from the problems that seemed to him the most important. Hence, by studying the differentiation of myths we may hope to discover something of the periods and races in which they were evolved. When Egypt had scarcely begun to make bricks, and Babylon as yet was but a village, already, it may be, the Dravidian hamlets of the south of India had received their consecration from the neighbourhood of the chosen block of unhewn stone outside their boundary, that remains to this day as the altar-place of Amma, the Infinite Mother. And only a palæolithic age, one imagines, could have suggested, as the ideal symbol, the low sharp-pointed cone of unchiselled rock that is worshipped still beneath the *neem*. But if this is so, we have in that very fact some indication of the earliest of human sociological developments. In the present age we instinctively ascribe to deity the aspect of masculinity. This is because our society is patriarchal and man dominant. There was an age, however, when woman alone was the steadfast unit; when marriage was an affair of an hour, and the child belonged to his mother's village; when all the men of that village were her brothers, the *mamas*, and natural defenders of her children; when marriage was only lawful between men and women of different villages; and when woman was the obvious head and governor of the whole. On such a society, raised to the highest point of organisation and efficiency, were based the origins of the ancient Egyptian monarchy, the government of Babylon, and the present royal family of Travancore in Southern India. In such a society, moreover, it was as natural to call God *She*, as it seems now to us to do the very opposite. Grey-haired women, full of strange lore about beasts and herbs, with deep wise eyes and gentle sovereignty of manners, were its ideal. Such were the Norns, the three grey Fates, who watered the ash-tree Yggdrasil night and morning with water drawn from the Ocean of Memory, turning all that it touched to snowy whiteness. Yet Yggdrasil was of a later age than the Indian *neem*, for one of its mighty roots was fixed in heaven, beneath the throne of Æsir, the Great God, where he and the Norns held court and judged the world. We have here the myth of a day when man has made himself king, and woman already stands subordinated.

The worship of the *neem* has its centre in Oude and Behar, the ancient Kosala and Magadha. From this it spreads north and south, to the deserts of Sind and the Dekkan. I have even seen it in the extreme south, in a beautiful glen near Salem. There the tree stood, in a sacred enclosure, shut in by a massive wall of grey stone some five or six feet in height. Under it a pot was buried, bottom upwards, making a dome-shaped object, and here and there around the little court were tiny boat-shaped lamps for ceremonial lighting. In Sind they go to great trouble and expense, it is said, to obtain the blessed tree, and plant it beside some well in the desert country, there to become the nucleus of a small artificial oasis. Only in East Bengal can I find no trace of its worship except as the home of Sitola Devi. The *aswattha* there surpasses it in sanctity, and servants from that country have a notion that it is haunted; and to see the spirit that dwells in it they hold a sign of approaching death.

Another proof of the great age of the *neem* as a sacred tree lies in the manner of the worship that is offered by women. It is common, in later Hinduism, to perform the ceremony of *pradakshina*, or circumambulation, as an act of reverence, and this is what we might have expected to find in the worship of a tree. But it is not what happens. Before the *neem* stands its fragment of rude stone, and in parts of the country where this vividly suggests the presence of the All-Mother, high-caste women go in bands, on certain moonlight nights, to offer the lights and sandal-paste, the sweetmeats and libations of milk, that constitute the necessary offerings. When this has been done they make themselves into a ring, and go round and round—not the stone, and not the tree, but—a handful of fire, on which incense is thrown, standing in front of the sacred stone. As they go they sing marriage-songs, mentally praying, probably, for the birth of children, and finally the party breaks into groups for the enjoyment of games, romping and singing. We have here a trace of those primitive seasonal dances that were the communal form of marriage. We have also a hint of how early the witness of the fire was invoked as essential to marriage. How far may we trust this suggestion as to the order of emergence of the great religious motives, such as fire, planets, earth, and the rest?

The *neem* may be worshipped at any time, by a woman who has first served the community to the extent of feeding ten beggars. But its greatest festivals occur on the moonlight nights of *Sravan* and *Bhadra*, August and September. The ceremony of *Tij* takes place on the third night of the new moon of *Sravan*, or August. On this day, it is considered extremely auspicious that young married women should receive gifts of clothes, jewels, or sweetmeats from their husband's mothers. When the presents arrive, the girl calls her friends and companions, and they go out into the moonlight, to bathe, put on the new possessions, worship at the feet of the *neem*, and then spend hours in free and boisterous merriment. On these occasions it is strictly correct to be accompanied by the boys and young men of their own village, and to be joined by them in the games which follow. Nor is this difficult to understand, for the night represents a return to the old festivities of the communal wedding, when the men of a girl's own village were regarded as her brothers and the idea of marriage with one of them could not occur. Here we have the equivalent of the May-Day games of Europe, and even the idea, spread by the Church, that May is an unlucky month for marriage, stands accounted for in the desire to extinguish heathen rites.

It was, as Hewitt has pointed out, this same age that gave to the position of the *mama*, or mother's brother, the strength which it still holds in Hindu society. He is essential at weddings, and it is he who must give the baby its first rice when six months old, thus accepting it as lawfully born of his own kindred. But the millenniums that have rolled by since the communal marriages of the matriarchate are shown in the fact that to perform this ceremony the mother's brother must now come to the house of the child's father.

In the memory of communal marriages, then, before the tree of the Great Mother, may lie the explanation of the Norse belief that Askr, the first man, was born of the ash. The choice of the months for these marriages was obviously dictated by the Indian climate, requiring that children should be born in the heat of the year, when the granaries would be full and the need of labour least. Even now, it is doubtless for the birth of sons that wives and mothers pray before the *neem*. For how many thousands of years have they sanctified their own brooding love in such spots, beneath the growing moon, ere the All-Mother has sent to the house a new man-child!

To the threshold of history we are carried back by this worship of the *neem*. It is night, the time that to primitive man was fraught with coolness and joy and formed the basis of all time-reckoning. About us sleep the southern forests. Long ago, if it was ever set there, the dim light has burned out before the stone at the foot of the sacred tree. Man is still a hunting animal, contending with hairier beasts for his simple home. A few rude stone implements, a little sun-dried pottery, and the struggling crops of half-wild rice, are all his possessions. Has he yet found fire? If so, for lamp-oil, as well as for medicine, he must still come to the sacred tree. Even his marriage is not yet his own: he knows only his sisters' children. Yet already here, in India, human society has been born. Already the lawful and lawless have been distinguished. Already the thought of enfolding Power has emerged. Already the sweetness of motherhood has been named. Already, in the sanctification of boundaries, the civic thought is born. Already the stone before the holy tree indicates a Presence the touch of whose feet makes sanctuary. Ages will go by, and man will long dream that the world is unchanging, ere these great movements will begin—north, east, and west—by which in the future nations and civilisations are to be made. Strange, that even now thoughts should have been conceived and expressed which will never be forgotten so long as man endures. Athene with her olive, and the Norns of the ash tree Yggdrasil are even now predestined to their place in human history, already in the forests of the Dekkan, in this the Palæolithic Age.

THE DREAD SEVEN

BENEATH the *neem* they sit, as did the Norns of old beneath *Yggdrasil*—those seven dread sisters, of whom Sitola, goddess of Smallpox, is the first. All the rashes and eruptions they share amongst them, and the youngest of the seven is the old friend of our childhood, no less a personage than Measles herself. It is strange, we feel, this element of fear that seems so often associated in ancient mythology with the idea of femininity. Head of the Fates is she who cuts the thread of life, and all the three are womenkind. Ate, the sleepless doom that pursues after the shedder of blood, is a woman. The Harpies and avenging Erinys are daughters, not sons, of the gods and of Night. And here in India the power that is seen in the burning of fever and the wasting of disease is conceived as the presence within a man of the Mother Herself.

The fact is an added token of the antiquity of the association. When the administration of justice took the form of a curse or a vendetta, pronounced by the grey-haired women of the village; when all power was as yet in the hands of the Mothers, and men were at best but their fierce and courageous children; when rulership could not be conceived of apart from the feminine —thus early awoke the idea of the divinity that is seen in the terrible and the irrevocable. Among peoples whose geographical compactness and comparative density hastened their political differentiation, the terror was more apt to take the form of a reflection of the fear of man and his just wrath. Righteous punishment was a thing to be looked for. The avenger of blood was most to be dreaded of all foes. But in India, that land of vast spaces and extended populations, the ideal of malign power remained mysterious, incalculable, and supernatural. From the beginning there was something inexplicable in the exercise of omnipotence. Could any sign of divine presence be more convincing, because more incomprehensible, than the spells of fever, or the anger of a rash? Naturally, then, the practice of worship developed the opposite power, that of healing.

Very quaint are the descriptions given by the faithful of the Seven Fearsome Sisters. That Smallpox makes affrighted goes without saying. Her power is open and irrepressible, afflicting men at noonday. But each one, even the youngest, has a potency of her own. Being the youngest, indeed, gives to Measles, it is said, a peculiar ability to do mischief. Her very age makes her the pet of her father and mother. She is therefore much indulged. She lives suppressed: that is to say, she is apt to exercise her powers in secret, and to leave behind her when she goes some terrible memento of her visit, in a permanent blindness, deafness, or lameness. It is evident here that a good deal of fine medical observation has been put into the curious old myth of the seven sisters.

It would be strange, however, if so careful an index of diagnosis were entirely dissociated from all consideration of methods of treatment. As we might have expected, the priests of Sitola come from a peculiar caste, being known as Dom Brahmins, and are, in fact, doctors of a very ancient order. The oldest worships are connected with libations, the pouring-out of water before God; but in the worship of Sitola the idea of a sanative cleanliness is very prominently brought forward. One will sometimes, in the by-ways of some busy city, see women after nightfall pouring out water in the road before a temple and sweeping the place with a broom. They are praying to Sitola, the guide will tell us. For those who know have laid down the law that this goddess demands salutation with water and a broom. Indeed she clasps these in her own arms as represented in her images; and she comes to us, they say, riding on the washerman's donkey, an unclean beast. In this last point, though undeniably forcible, public opinion is probably wrong. Sitola is represented, it is true, as riding on an ass, but in all likelihood this is because, in that remote past out of which she rose, the ass was the fleet courser, the splendid and romantic steed, hero of all the poetry that now centres in the horse. He may, in an age of degeneration, be relegated to the use of the laundryman's caste, daily parading the town with his load of soiled linen for the wash. But he is most emphatically one of those who have seen better days. Once upon a time he held a ruling position amongst animals, and in the Semitic races his appearance in a procession would seem to have indicated semi-royal state as late as the opening of the Christian era. Wild in the deserts of Arabia, he appears in the liturgy of ancient Egypt as the Sun-god, and scholars hold that traces of this identification may still be found in the *Rig-Veda* itself. Even now there is a breed in Persia which is famous and honoured, transcending even the horse in swiftness, and making it seem in no wise ludicrous that a goddess should be seated on an ass.

Many students will feel that the assignment of one whole divinity to the province of a single disease argues a state of society in which there was a very elaborate division of labour. Nor can we help connecting this advance in social organisation with that sudden accession of medical science of which the worship of Sitola constitutes a remnant. The whole idea is a rare mixture of piety and wisdom. When the patient first succumbs to the malady, there is many a village-wife whose diagnosis is as valuable as the physician's or the priest's. The one anxiety is that the eruption should have free way. Should it remain suppressed, the case is regarded as grave. But if this is not so, and matters appear promising, the next step is to feed with a sufficient quantity of milk. The amount of this food that can be digested by a smallpox patient of robust constitution is said to be quite incredible. If the case is bad, however, there is nothing to be done but call for the special attendance of a priest of Sitola. In this case the sick man will be laid on the floor on cool banana leaves. He is also given medicine brought by the priest. A twig of *neem* is supplied to him, and except with it he is not allowed to touch his own skin. To tickle it with the sacred twig is an invocation of blessing. At the same time devotions are going on. At first, when the fell visitant was announced, the women of the household repaired in the evening to temple or tree, to offer their worship. Part of this consisted in placing flowers on top of an inverted pot, at the feet of the goddess. If the flowers fall, she is pleased, and grants the prayer of her suppliant. But if they remain where they were placed, she is obdurate, and the end can hardly be bright. I have been told of one case in which the women had placed their flowers and sat in the attitude of prayer to see what was to be their fate. The blossoms did not fall, and in agony of mind the whole party bent still lower in prayer, imploring with clasped hands that the Devi might take pity and grant a life much loved. At this second prayer, as they watched and waited, the flowers fluttered down, slowly, slowly, and each one felt that an invisible hand had taken them, and the prayer would be fulfilled.

Only half the necessary offering is thus made, however. The idea, in Bengal at least, is that the Mother has been asked to visit the abode of her children and bless them with a healing touch. This is the element in the myth to which prominence is given, though it is not quite clear that there is not mixed with it an older notion that it is the presence of the goddess that has brought disaster, and that she is being begged to withdraw. Outside Bengal this last seems to be frankly the thought. But here we are mainly in the attitude of entreating the Mother to enter the house and bear away its misfortune. The more archaic fear may be traced in the fact that, while the illness remains, none in the house will venture to call it by any name but "the mercy." And the visitors who generally throng to see an invalid remain here, it is true, on the threshold; but still they come, saying they are adoring the divine Mother, present in the sick. So the conception of the healing divinity of sweetness has not yet wholly emancipated itself from an older and less noble worship of fear; but it is on the way to do so, for when the recovery has taken place it is always unhesitatingly attributed to a visit of benediction, and many are the household tales of special experiences illustrating this. From the moment of the announcement, then, when the worship is offered, the house and everyone in it has to be kept in a state of such exceptional purity as is meet for those who expect a divine advent. No meat or fish may be cooked within the walls. Only after bathing, and wearing the cleanest of garments, may the sick be attended. Fresh flowers and incense are to be offered daily. Water and the broom must do even more than their ordinary work in constant cleansing. And finally, when the last remnant of his illness is well past, the patient marks his own recovery by a delightful bath, for which he has been prepared by massage, being rubbed with sandal-paste and turmeric, ancient luxuries of the toilet, full of coolness and fragrance.

The sons of Askr, or the ash, carried into Europe,

it is said, the use of bronze, the domesticated horse, and also the knowledge of massage and of healing drugs and oils. We have seen that the horse must have been subjugated by man and have reached the world's great trade-routes at Babylon and Nineveh only after the ass had been long familiar. We know also that it must have come from Central Asia, and the probability is that it had been tamed long enough before the memorising of the present *Rig-Veda* for its predecessor to be even then, amongst the Aryans, only a dim and half-conscious tradition. That Sitola and her sisters should number seven in all shows that they were the creation of some race in whom astronomic studies and planetary lore had already made the number seven peculiarly sacred and impressive, as it was among the singers of the Vedas. They appear also, on comparing their characters with those of the corresponding fear-creating goddesses of Europe, to belong to a civilisation in which political and military ideas were slower of growth and personal culture a larger factor. Bronze is held by some scholars to have been the result of the exchange of copper at Tamralipti or Tamluk, with the tin of Malacca, in the ages of the Asiatic merchant-civilisation, which preceded the rise of nationalities. In Asia, as also among the nomads of North America, there seems to have been a short Copper Age preceding the Bronze. Copper razors and copper axes have been found in India, and copper knives on the site of ancient Troy. After this came bronze, and with bronze, as far as Europe was concerned, the knowledge of medicine and the use of the horse. Older, far older, than any of these, was that worship of the rude stone beneath the *neem* tree, as the throne of the Mother, and those seasonal dances that may have given rise to the tradition of the birth of Askr, the first man, from the ash. Holy indeed is the ground beneath the olive and the *neem*. Sacred homes of the Oil-Mother, from them and their long past has come every notion of priestly anointing that a younger world has seen. The chrism of baptism, the oil of coronation, and the last sad rite of unction and benediction to the forth-going soul—here, in the cool breeze that blows through our Indian tree of healing, may have been the birth of all these, and of how much more throughout the ages of aid and fellowship between man and man.

THE KASHMIR SHAWL

THE glory has departed from Srinagar, for it is now some eighteen centuries since the city, under a Buddhist sovereign, was capital of the greater part of India. But if the ancient glory has vanished, a new and greater has come in its stead. The quaint old town is to-day the centre of some of the chief art industries of the world, and among other things, it is the home of the Kashmir Shawl. The Tartars brought the art of shawl-weaving into the country about four or five centuries ago; then it came under the stimulating influence of Indian taste, and developed rapidly from a domestic handicraft into a fine art. To this day the goats' wool which it requires is brought from Yarkand to Srinagar, and only the young fleece of the first year is considered fine enough for use.

Three brains combine to produce this work of art. First comes the designer, who receives a couple of shillings for his trouble; next the copier, who prepares the pattern for use in the workshop, and last of all the weaver. Of these, the second is regarded as most skilled and receives five times the remuneration bestowed on the original artist. To us this seems a pity. That a genius should be regarded as a mere workman, lost in the crowd of mediocrity, is shocking to us. Besides, we lose thereby all that charm of personality that clings to a toy-book by Hokusai, for instance, or a bit of modelling by the Della Robbias. But there is much to be said on behalf of a certain custom that withdraws all the degrading if stimulating influence of Fame, and leaves to the worker only that highest compelling power of the artistic conscience. Such conditions pass all too quickly. They belong to the great age of Faith all over the earth, and with their decay comes loss of purity and tension to all save the noblest souls. Besides, as a matter of skill the gradation is not so absurd after all, for the taste is not mere transference of line and tint, but the translation of those into musical score.

The weaver actually possesses no copy of the design except in this notation. The manuscript of a melody lies in front of him, and from this he weaves the pattern that we see. A Kashmiri loom is really a little orchestra, and each shawl a symphony of colours, the men as they work chanting the stitches in monotonous plain-song. The connection between colour and sound is fundamental in Indian art-fabrics—though the point has never been investigated so far as we know—

and furnishes the key to that power of combining and harmonising in which they are supreme.

It is to these copyists that experts must look for the restoration of the old patterns which cannot at present be repeated. It is by them, too, that the material will be produced which must eventually be brought together to form a national museum. At present there are no records kept of these marvellous decorative schemes, and no collections save those made by dealers in the interest of their trade. Even then, however, there is abundant opportunity for studying the progress of the art, and no chance of escaping its spell.

Comparing the shawls of two hundred years ago with those of to-day, we find in the modern specimens a greater boldness and freedom of outline, with a growing power of colour-combination. From purely geometrical means there is distinct movement towards conventionalising vegetal forms —the monotonous curves (a local variation of the Indian pine-pattern) and circles giving place in great measure to trailing tendrils and spiral ornaments. The Moslem faith forbids any imitation of animal forms: hence we find none of the beautiful birds of Kashmir, the hoopoe, the bulbul, or the blue kingfisher, amongst these flowers. With regard to colour, the development of power has been extraordinary. A few of the old shawls are incomparably fine, but on the whole the number of shades used in masterpieces was far smaller than those commonly manipulated now. The achievements of William Morris in this line give some idea to the English mind of the kind of text employed. But the cretonnes and tapestries of Merton are coarse and almost clumsy compared with these exquisite stuffs.

Indian taste demands three things of the decorator: fineness of detail, brilliance of effect, and profuseness. This is natural in a climate which produces the beautiful in splendid masses without relief or pause. It is the flower-jewelled villages of Kashmir that are reflected in the national industries, just as it was the luxuriance of the jungle that trained hands and eyes to build the Taj and perforate the marble at Ahmedabad.

It is worth while to remember that the selfsame cause which gives its dazzling beauty to Oriental ornament makes Western art a fine vehicle for the impression of ideas. Our walls are ugly, yet we have fine sculptures, a Raphael, and a Rossetti. We have no gorgeous palaces maybe, but what of our grey cathedrals? The world would be as much poorer for the loss of an old English village church as by the further destruction of the rose-red walls of Delhi; but on the other hand we must not forget that the porcelains of China and the mosaics of Agra are just as essential to the whole as the ruined cloisters of Europe or the regal architecture of Westminster and Versailles. The great rhythm of Time and Space in which the Indian mind so delights finds once more an illustration here. Not in the Good alone, but also in the Evil, in Death as well as Life, in the West and in the East, in diversity of all kinds, is to be read the revelation of Unity. From all points do the paths converge by which the One comes to the vision of man.

Shawl-making, then, is to-day a living industry in this Central Asian valley of its birth, but we cannot deny that the modern craftsman works under corrupting influences unknown to his forefathers. The last twenty years have opened up the beautiful vale to European intercourse, and the disastrous effects of fashion and semi-education are as apparent here as in the ancient arts of wood-carving and *papier-maché*. If the Kashmir weaver is to be saved at all from denationalised vulgarity, it can only be by a close and sympathetic study of the old masterpieces, and by the careful enlightenment of Western taste.

The fall of the last French Empire dealt a death-blow to the use of the shawl, from which it will probably never recover; but the recognition of these exquisite garments as tapestries and furniture draperies is inevitable with the advance of knowledge and discrimination amongst us. This is bound to supersede the square outline by the panel and other forms, and may, it is much to be feared, have many less salutary consequences. Hence it is important that such losses should be balanced by still greater gains of freedom, originality, and bewildering loveliness—and, as all will agree, these must be in the spirit of the old work, to the exclusion of incongruous elements, if they are to signify development and not deterioration.

This fine industry has a primitive air all through. The pedlar is the great agent of dissemination, and in dealing with him the process of bartering needs to be treated as a science. In his own fastnesses, down in the bazaar, the unwary buyer is at a grave disadvantage, for tea is served in dainty old china, and all the honeyed resources of Oriental courtesy are exhausted to make the obligation more complete. So in Cairo, sitting in the shop-sill drinking coffee out of egg cups, it costs the whole afternoon to spend ten shillings.

But if the ramifications of the trade strike us as quaint in their simplicity, what shall we think of those little factories in which the manufacture is carried on?

In a tiny mud-built cottage, baked silver-grey by the sun's heat—one of a number surrounding the irregular farmyard-square that to the Indian mind represents the slum—in an upper room which also contains a bed, we may find three looms, set at right angles to the windows, and giving space altogether to nine workers. Their monotonous weavers' chant ceases as we enter and fingers fall idle, that we may be free to examine the machines at our pleasure. These long low frames are comparatively small, and stretched across from back to front lie the close tight strands of the warp. Such a work as it is! Long delicate threads of creamy white or glistening grey, or some wonderful shade of green or rose or blue. It is the hair of young goats, in its first downy softness, spun almost to the thinness of spider silk.

Equally fine are more coloured wools—wound on little spindles instead of reels—which the men take up and with incredible swiftness (reading the manuscript before them with their voices and *listening* to the pattern with their fingers, as it were) pass in and out, over and under, through the background, counting as they work. And so without gleam of shuttles or noise of machinery, line upon line, stitch after stitch, by the patient labour of human fingers grows the web of the Kashmir shawl. Overhead hangs a row of brilliantly-dyed skeins of yarn. It is the gamut of colours in which the design is pitched and deepens the analogy to the symphony in music. Now, as the men yield once more to that abstracting power which all needlework, and specially all darning, possesses, breaking out into a louder strain, we realise afresh that this relationship of sound which the ear appreciates so easily is identical with that which appeals only to the eye. We are reading our pattern through two senses at once.

Truly this is a craft of olden times. Witness the fact that every one of the processes may be carried on under the same roof. Down yonder in the courtyard, in the shadow of the thick wall, sit three women who, in their statuesque Kashmiri beauty, might be the Greek Fates—in the middle the grandmother, with her spinning-wheel, and beside her two daughters-in-law, pulling and twisting the yet untinted fleece. The quiet dignity of age surrounds the old Moslem woman. The face under the veil and coronet is as of one who has loved and suffered and triumphed like a queen. Ask her her faith, and note the ring in her voice as she answers proudly: "Praise be to God! Thanks to the mercy of the Lord, I am a Mussulman!" "The mercy of the Lord" and the banner that we associate with sword and slaughter!

But the children play on unheeding in the sunshine, the wheel turns merrily, and through the open window above us floats the song of the men at their weaving. It is indeed a note from a far past age, and as we stand, looking and listening, we think we hear those words from an Eastern book, "Man's days are swifter than a weaver's shuttle."

But yesterday, the Tartars entered Srinagar,

to-day the English are here, and to-morrow they will be gone, leaving an old old race to dream once more the sweet dreams of labour and poetry and beauty, till—as they themselves would phrase their hope—the net of Maya shall be broken and they be lost in the ocean of the Beatific Vision.

THE LAND OF THE WATER-WAYS

THERE is no region, even in India, which was intended to compare, at once in extent and in fertility, with the wide-stretching delta-lands of East Bengal. Placed between the extreme mouth of the Ganges and the Brahmaputra, from Calcutta on the west to Chittagong on the east, and Dacca and Mymensingh on the north, lies this vast triangle of country, measuring, as the crow flies, something like two hundred miles or more every way. And it is painted on the surface of planet Earth in nature's most vivid pigments of green and blue. Green for the fields and forests, the palms and the gardens and the grain; and blue, blue, blue everywhere else, for the sky above and for the waters beneath. To those who know Holland, or even Venice, this land is full of subtle suggestions and reminiscences of distant beauty. For it, too, is a country snatched from the waters, though not by the hand of man. It, too, lies passive and half-expectant under the unbroken dome of heaven. In it, too, the white sail may suddenly come into vision at any moment across the distant meadows. And it, too, bestows that irresistible calmness of benediction that comes to the infinitely small in the presence of the infinitely great.

There are of course differences. This is a tropical Holland. The wide green flats are broken, not by stiff avenues of poplars and rows of wintry pollard elms, but by long irregular fringes of jungle, groups of cocoanut and betel-nut palms, clusters of delicate bamboos, outstanding leaf-almonds here and there, with almost every branch of glossy verdure ending in a leaf like a scarlet flag, and lines of upright banana plants, hedging in the fruit and vegetable gardens of the homesteads. These last, too, are, as is natural, strangely different from the prim farmhouses of the Dutch with their red tiles. From the river-front we see a large thatched roof, whose wide curving eaves overhang a cottage built apparently of something like basket-work, but in fact of mats, woven out of bamboo-splinters. The rafters and posts of this simple structure are also of bamboo, and it may be that a single roof covers, not only the home, but also a small open barn, holding a couple of cows, while over the heads of these last is seen again a second storey with floor made of split bamboo, and filled with rice-straw, thus answering all the purposes of a hayloft. The floor of the cottage itself, in any case, is made of clean silver river-clay, packed solid and tight and smooth. And a very good test of the wealth of the family lies in the height of this modern plinth. Within, the dwelling has in all probability a ground-floor, lifted a foot or two above this of mud, and made, like that of the hayloft, of split-bamboo; and on this, with whatever they may be able to command of comfort in the way of cushions, wadded sheets, and cotton carpets, the household live. The one large room is often partitioned into two or three smaller. Always there is an open veranda outside which acts as the family reception-room. Almost always there is some corner, either in but or ben, which is built off from the rest, and used as the cooking room. And in every house there are wooden and bamboo platforms overhead, which can be used either as store-cupboards or extra sleeping rooms, according as the special occasion demands. The little farmhouse, however, has no doorway of inferior dignity. Even when the front entrance is towards the river bank, it is nevertheless almost certain that the open veranda will be found on the far side, facing, like a simple cloister, the interior of the little farmyard, on the two or three other sides of which are placed similar, but probably still less imposing, dwellings. Here, too, are the outbuildings and offices of the farm, the husking-shed, the cow-house, the dovecote, and the feeding-place for ducks, with close at hand the herb and fruit garden. And the whole of this little group of reed-built chambers is enclosed and connected with the next like it by the homestead grove of palms and jungle-growth. It has its own boat, too, made of long narrow planks of palm wood, in which seven or eight people can sit in single file, so long as one or two remain constantly busied, baling out the water with which it is as constantly filling. And finally, this cluster of houses does not constitute a village. It may take twenty or more of such, thrown like the links of a chain around and across the rice fields, to make a single village-community. Hence, in this wonderful country, it is sometimes possible, sitting in the low boat of the water-lanes, to say that the village includes more than the horizon.

In the riverside villages, again, the *Chashas*, or peasants, and the *Majhis*, boatmen or fisherfolk, dwell side by side. They are for the most part Mohammedans and only sometimes Hindus. But the two do not always live in separate villages. Nor is there any great difference between them in point of civilisation. A few hundreds of years ago all alike were Hindus, but to the low castes, Islam, with its message of democracy and brotherly love, offers a great emancipation. And in East Bengal these must have been swept into the fold, whole villages at a time. The descendants of such converts have the title "Sheikh" prefixed to their names, and here they are all Sheikhs. But even now they appear like Hindus. Their widows are loath to remarry. They wear the unbordered *sari* and cut the hair short, like the Hindu widow. They object to cow-killing, like the Hindus. Their children are trained, not in the knowledge of the Koran alone, but also in the stories of the old Indian epics. And finally, their homes are decorated with the same religious pictures and images as those of the Hindu. In other words, it is one race practising the forms of two different faiths, and even in India blood speaks louder than creed.

They are a proud and self-respecting folk, these people of the villages of East Bengal, decent and thrifty in all their ways, as conscious as ourselves of subtle differences of rank and education, and full of the spirit of independence and self-reliance. It is not easy here to buy the trifle to which one takes a fancy. Permission to do so may be asked with all possible formality and ceremony, but the answer is invariably the smiling surrender of the object, as a gift. I have a little boatman's lamp of black earthenware, which came to me in this way. It is one of the loveliest things I ever saw, and its value in the village-markets is, I am told, one farthing. But though I offered sixteen times that sum, its owner would not hear of purchase, insisting instead on presenting it to me. Of a similar significance was my first encounter with the Barisal fisher-folk. In this land of canals, it is customary to use for conveyance a very fine and commodious Indian form of house-boat. The empty rooms, made of dark polished teak-wood, are scrupulously clean, and we bring our own rugs and pillows, and sit or lie on the floor for the journey. Outside, under bamboo arches, covered with sliding hoods of reed mats, sit the boatmen. And a few fishing-nets, or a spindle with its thread, or a small clay stove at which cooking is going on, offer at once the only traces of furniture, and the only elements of picturesque disorder, to be seen. The crew consists of the men of a single family, from the grey-haired grandfather or grand-uncle to the youngest boy. The women have been left at home in the distant village, to tend the cows, and spin, and look after the gardens. There is something of the dignity of Homer's peasant-kings in such a scheme of life and work; and I was a little diffident with the first boatmen I had accosted, in making inquiries as to whether the prevailing famine and rise in prices had made themselves felt severely by them and theirs. Their first effort was to put me at my ease. Gravely and kindly they took up the question. Work, they said, had become scarce everywhere. No one who could possibly do without it would employ labour at such a time. Everyone naturally was cutting his expenses down. They themselves, for instance, had lain to, at the little quay where we found them, for ten days past, and this was the first day they had been employed. Inevitably, therefore, things were a little difficult. But they had managed. Oh yes! they had managed. And they had no doubt that in some way or other they would contrive to go on. With this abrupt reserve, this lowering of the visor, so to speak, the subject was dropped, and could be pursued no further. Yet it was not that the newcomer had been rebuked for impertinence, but rather that all alike we had realised the sudden pain of the attempt to lay bare our necessities to others.

And everywhere in the famine-villages I found the same thing. Here and there as we went about, we would come upon someone whose store of money or provisions was not yet wholly exhausted, someone who was still hoping that public charity would prove unnecessary to his little household. And wherever this happened the personal question would be skilfully evaded, and any discussion of the situation quietly refused. It is needless to say that the intense sensitiveness and delicacy of these Indian villagers played its own part in helping to deepen our understanding of the prevailing desolation. Every story told meant so much pride overcome.

Like a great net made of cords of shining silver-blue, the water-ways—broad rivers, narrower canals or *khals*, and narrowest of all the little water-lanes—hold lovingly in their clasp this beautiful land, which throughout the historic period has been known as the Granary of Bengal. But the villages have a proverb, "With kings, with horned beasts, and with a river a man may never be friends." Much as the heart may go out in love, that is to say, there will surely come sooner or later, with such, a moment of treachery, when they will deal out death to him whom they have caressed. Alas, that this should have proved true of our lovely rivers of East Bengal.

Already the villages had been many months in the grip of famine. For the chief Indian harvest of the year is reaped in January, and in this year of 1906 it was terribly scant. The rains twelve months ago, at the time of sowing, were too little. Moreover, in some of the more ocean-exposed districts there were salt floods, and the crops were ruined. Within a month or two of this year's reaping, therefore, the long slow agony of starvation must have set in amongst the people. But it was borne in grim silence as long as possible, and only in the middle of June did the terrible word Famine make itself heard. And yet, as if the cup of their sorrows were not even now full, it became clear, on the breaking of the monsoon, that the rains this year were to be excessive; and finally, in the middle of August, the rivers, swollen by heavy rains and melting snows in the far north, suddenly broke their bounds, and the fair lands of Eastern Bengal became a world under water, the floods doubling the disaster created by the famine.

I.—Famine and Flood

It was dawn on the 8th of September; one of those dawns of pearl and opal that come to us in the Indian autumn. The water-lilies lay open still, as they had lain all night long on the surface of the waters. Here we paddled up to a cluster, lying touching one another, as if with their heads on each other's shoulders, with golden hearts, and rose-tinged petals. And we counted them and found them seven. Seven lilies open in the dawn! The air was cool but not chill, and full of quiet and fragrance. And all around us in every direction—inwards from the edge of the river-current behind us, to the distant line of farmstead groves, and right and left, all the way from one dark jungle-border to another—stretched the smooth silver water, pierced by the upspringing spears of the young rice, which here and there was so scanty that each upright blade was companioned by its own reflection in the water-mirror underneath. A world full of the joy of the senses—

not a gross or physical delight, but the silent in-flooding of sense-rapture on the spirit—for him whose body was fed and mind at rest.

A world of sense-joy. Was that how it looked to the women yonder, standing up to their waists in water, to receive us, as we paddled and punted towards their dwelling-place? Much sense-joy feel these others, think we, who have taken refuge with their children, from their fallen house, in the hay-loft of a neighbour, and are living there, more like birds than human beings—who can tell us how many days? Nay, for these, and their like, there can be no joy of the senses, for the present is to them a horror, and who knows what agony may await them in the near future?

Or it was noon, and in a distant part of the country, not very far in fact from the city, we waded in water above the knees, or shot in the palm-boat across the rice-fields, finding our way from one farmhouse to another. And still, in spite of the sorrow all about us, one could now and then only catch one's breath, and feel how wondrous, to him who was born amongst them, must be the brimful beauty of these rice-lands. Grey clouds, grey mists, grey waters, and drizzling rain, we seemed to be alone in a world-vastness, alone, alone. Suddenly a great wind would catch the jungle-belt about us, and all the mangoes and palms respond, moaning and wailing. Then again it would pass, and silence come once more, upon the infinite monotony of our level world, with the first sense back, of a fulness of something that was neither life nor death, but on the mystic border-line between the two—perhaps including both.

Never have I felt so strongly the oneness of the people the world over as a few days ago, when I was allowed to begin my famine visits by calling at one farmhouse after another in the district on the opposite bank of the river to the town of Barisal. Some of these famine-stricken dwellings belonged to *Chashas*, or peasant-labourers—men, that is to say, who are employed as farm-hands, at a daily or monthly wage. And there were besides these the houses of the well-to-do tenant farmers, brought low like all the rest in this year of desolation by the very extremity of economic disaster.

For we cannot say in India, as we might perhaps in Ireland, that the higher classes live on one food, and the lower on another. There is here no contrast, as of wheat and potatoes, so that one half of the village may experience the last pangs of hunger while the other flourishes on the abundance of its own crop. All over the Gangetic Plain and all over the Gangetic Delta (and it is convenient to speak of all the rivers of these parts, whatever their local names, as the Ganges) all classes alike live on rice.

And when rice fails them all alike starve. The employer of labour can, of course, hold out longer than the labourer he employs, in the battle against want. He ought to have something in the way of money and jewels. He has house, tools, furniture, and cattle that can (though it is to no one's interest that they should) be sold. He has even, if the worst should come to the worst, a larger credit. And he uses it to the utmost. If a man be found without resources in a year of supremely scanty harvest, we may be sure that it will prove to be because he had already parted with home and land in the former years, when ill-fortune was only growing upon him.

One home there was that I visited that morning, in which I would fain hope to have made permanent friends. Its mistress was a young woman, some few years widowed, whose grown-up son was the breadwinner of the family. At the hour of our visit he was absent, seeking employment, and they would have nothing to cook that day unless he should return with rice. Not that this was stated or obtruded upon our notice. Rather we came to understand the fact when our visit was past. Meanwhile, we sat and chatted quietly in the closely-thatched veranda, and one noted a daughter of the household, a girl of twelve or fourteen, clad with the scantiness of the year's poverty, and sore of heart under the wound to her girlish pride. There was a grey-haired granddame too, who told us, not of the famine but of the deep abiding sorrow that all other pain was wont to renew in her—the memory of the deaths, long ago, of seven stalwart sons who had each grown to man's estate before, one by one, they left her, to wait alone for the word of Allah ere she might see them again in Paradise. A widowed neighbour crept in to talk and listen, carrying a girl-baby in an extreme of emaciation, whom she was trying to nurse back into life, its own mother being dead. But centre of all was the gentle mistress of the home. One could gather her past happiness from the story she told of the debts of the dead husband faithfully discharged, and by her sensitive shrinking from the thought of remarriage. Even as we sat talking her son came back from the city and handed to his mother a bag containing some four pounds of rice, earned by two days of labour, carrying bricks on the river in a boat. Work, he said, was absolutely at a standstill, and one gathered from his words the fear he did not utter, of the days when he must return empty-handed from such quests. What would then be the fate of these helpless ones of his kindred who were dependent on him for food?

The cheery old Hindu gentleman who accompanied me in my visits would not, however, allow any presentiment of coming evil. "Come, come, Lakshmi!" (Fortuna), he said soothingly to the mother, who, weakened by long fasting, was weeping quietly and silently. "We shall send you help—do not you fear! And better times will be with us shortly—There, there! Don't forget! The good days will come again." Like the captain of the ship in stormy weather, it was not to the women he would admit the anxiety that was weighing upon his own kind heart, with the thought of the awful month of October to November, when the money contributed by the country and the last rice held by the starving people would alike be exhausted and heaven alone could tell where he would have to look for help.

The weeping woman dried her eyes and silently strove for self-control. And then with the prayers and blessings of the aged Rizpah ringing in our ears, we rose to leave for the boats that awaited us. But down to the edge of the water-meadows came the women to see us off. And there with my last look backwards I saw them standing, their hands raised in the attitude of prayer. And I knew that they, in their want and anxiety, were giving to us, well-fed and well-clothed, the beautiful salutation of their people, "Peace be unto you!"

II.—The Commonwealth based on Rice

How futile, when one has seen a famine, sound all discussions as to whether or not India in the past has known as great catastrophes! A fair mansion, standing on the side of a great river, suddenly falls in a year of flood, and what remains of it henceforth is only a ruin. The house fell the moment the waters reached a certain level. Yes; but it would not have fallen at such a touch, only that, during long years before, the underpinnings and foundations had been steadily snapped and undermined. The final calamity was only the last scene in a drama of disaster long proceeding in silence. And the house itself could never have been built under such conditions. That is the whole argument. The commonwealth was never built up under such conditions.

Everything that one sees in East Bengal to-day is so much saved from happier times. Is it the pride and independence of fisher-folk and farmers? Is it the delicate hospitality of starving villagers? Both alike, if the present strain continue long enough, must assuredly give way to a sordid pauperism. They could never, under such disadvantages, have sprung into being. No, the ruin wrought by fire, or earthquake, or tidal wave, may happen in an hour. But famine implies a long train of preparatory circumstances, with which a bad season, or a series of bad seasons, suddenly coincides, to work visible devastation. That a certain combination of bad seasons must necessarily recur in every century or half-century will, I presume, appear a truism to the mathematician versed in the doctrines of chances. And that an agricultural civilisation of three thousand years' standing should be familiar with, and make provision for, the fact of such a recurrence, will appear equally a truism to the student of sociology.

It is in accordance with this fact that the people of East Bengal have been in the habit of keeping always stored in their houses some two or three years' provision of rice at a time. All over India the family that is rich enough buys its rice for the month or the year by the *maund*, even as in England we buy coal by the ton.[1] But the farmer was supposed never to encroach, for the purposes of the market, upon the store of grain that was to secure food to his household and dependents, not only during the current year, but also during two scanty harvests ahead, should the country be so unfortunate as to experience these. Now those

A *maund* is about 80 lbs., *i.e.* about ⅞ cwt. It represents, as food, about 160 days for one person.

who have followed the story I am telling will at once perceive the necessity of this. The convention was etiquette. It was more, it was morality—*Dharmma*, the national righteousness. But it was more even than these: it was plain common-sense. For we have seen that the farmer who cannot pay for labour even under the agricultural mischance of a bad harvest (strictly parallel to a season of commercial or manufacturing debits instead of credits), must necessarily fall from the position of an employer of labour into that of the employee or day-labourer himself. Instead of a farmer, he is now a *Chasha* or ploughman merely. Food may return into the district, through relief associations or along the railways, but this is not the same thing as its returning into his hands. He has lost his social status, and it will be long before he can possibly regain it. The security of the farmer as a capitalist depends, then, upon this one thing, and upon it alone, that he keep in possession a three-years supply of rice. In districts in the close neighbourhood of Calcutta, where the houses of the peasants are built of more permanent materials than further east, I know of nothing more pathetic to see than the long array of village granaries, many of them structures of an exquisite beauty, empty.

The rise in the money value of food is sufficient to explain to us the impossibility for the East Bengal farmers, during recent years, of abiding by the injunction of their forefathers that they should keep rice in their granaries. They have lived in a world which regards it as more essential that they should keep money in their purse.

What have been the causes at work to transfer the peasant's ambition from rice to silver, from a well-filled granary to a well-filled till? For unless the ambition has been so transferred it is clear that the money value of grain could not have risen so rapidly. Only when a province has been denuded, and all its food has to be imported, could the crop of the country reach such values as those at present prevailing.

With regard to this question, it is perhaps sufficient to say that all over India a process is going on, in consequence of which the peasant has come to look upon money as wealth. And this process may be briefly indicated by the statement that rent and taxes have to be paid in coin. The foreign tax-gatherer, or the foreign minister of the Exchequer, knows nothing of rice as the ultimate standard of value. To them the precious metals occupy this place. And here is a fact which would tend of itself to impoverish the peasant, relatively to the other classes of the community, even if all the wealth of India remained within her own borders. The fact that it does not do so is too well known to need repetition at this point. My present object is merely to examine whether there be any local or little-known circumstances which may recently have contributed in some special measure to undermine the prosperity of East Bengal, and so have prepared the way for the calamity I have described.

Famine is social paralysis. A civilisation that has taken thousands of years to build up may be shattered by a single season of it. For complete destitution of all classes together, in a given area, is apt to knock out the links and rivets of the social system. At the present moment, for instance, the farmers have neither money nor food to give in exchange for labour. And without labour the rice of next year cannot be saved, even to the extent that might still have been possible. Under such circumstances, it is clear that food given to the farmer and his peasants is not the same thing as food given the farmer for his peasants. For in the latter case the food not only nourishes: it also leads to the putting in of labour, necessary to the next harvest. In the East there may be a greater readiness to return to the condition of equilibrium when the shock is over than in younger lands better known to ourselves. There may be: I do not know that there is, for I have not yet had the chance of seeing. But the difference can only at best be one of degree. Famine involves social disorganisation as one of its secondary but most far-reaching effects.

For famine is many things besides hunger. True, it is hunger so keen that one man whom I know, spending some days in a district as yet unrelieved, could not sleep at night for the wail of the famine-stricken in his ears. Hunger so keen, ah God! so keen! But it is more than this, as we have already seen. It is the extreme of poverty, bringing among other things nakedness, darkness at nightfall, ignorance, and unrepair in its train. It is poverty breeding poverty. Under its pressure the milk-cows are sold to the butcher, sometimes for eight annas or a shilling, because their owners can no longer maintain them, and by the new master are killed immediately for their hides, at the value of which he bought them. When it comes, the seed of the next year is eaten as food; the savings of lifetimes are scattered to the winds. Economic relationships thatseemed inherent in the social organism are broken to pieces.

But over and above even these things, famine is more. It is the very sickle of death, selecting its victims according to a certain invisible but predetermined order, and what that order is, it may be worth our while to inquire.

A few years ago there was a picture on exhibition in London, called, if I am not mistaken, "The Stairway of Life." At the top of wide-spreading steps stood youth and maiden hand-in-hand, and then, diverging with each step downwards, towards the river of death at the bottom, one saw the same pair, over and over again, at the different stages of life. This picture has been constantly in my mind as I have gone about the famine villages. Only the river of death that I see with the mind's eye is in flood, and at each step of the stairway stand the different grades of health and society, ranked according to the likelihood of their being swept off by the rising waters.

On the lowest stand the beggars, for every Indian community has its quota of these. There is here no poor-rate, and the hopelessly indigent and helplessly feeble must needs be supported by the informal charity of the village. Lonely old women they are for the most part, sunned and wrinkled under all weathers, and they stand at the steamer-*ghâts*, or in the bazaars, staff and begging-bowl in hand, not the least picturesque of all the picturesque elements that go to make up the Indian crowd.

Naturally, these are the first inhabitants of the villages to feel the sharp pinch of adversity, the first to throw themselves upon a wider-reaching charity. Indeed the Bengali word for famine, *durbhikkha*, the "hard begging," gives us a wonderful picture of the disaster from their point of view. It paints the beggars going forth in all directions, and wandering far ere they find scant food. Economic pauperism is a condition that only under very exceptional circumstances tends to bring out the highest and finest elements in human character, and these Indian beggars of the villages are neither better nor worse than their kind in other countries. Pithy and smart of repartee they sometimes are, and one cannot but be entertained when the grave assurance is given that the speaker dined yesterday on "horse's eggs" (a Bengali colloquialism for no food), in the very face of the person, it may be, who provided her with rice. It is undoubtedly true also that the beggar is spiritually twin-brother to the millionaire. For the minds of both these are concentrated upon the acquisition of wealth, in a degree impossible to any intermediate rank.

But the one lesson of my pilgrimage amidst the starving has been the immensity of the gulf that divides the humblest of citizens from these civic paupers. It takes a long series of scanty harvests to turn the poorest Indian householder into a beggar. Unless this is understood, we fail of the whole moral.

The next class to be reached by the rising

waters consists of the single women, respectable widows, and girls of their blood as yet unmarried, who have no one to work for them, and must make their own living by husking the rice of the farmers, and preparing it for the city-markets. These are the gleaners of Asiatic village-life: for they follow after the reapers at time of harvest, and by gathering the grain that falls in their wake, provide themselves with food for some one or two months out of every twelve. Theirs is thus the unbought store. Indeed, it is difficult to see how money ever passes through their hands, for the labour they give at rich farmhouses is paid in kind rather than in coin, and probably a piece of cloth from the farmer's wife on the great festivals meets their need of clothing for the year.

On the next level that the flood reaches are the homes of the peasants, the farm-labourers. And last of the village group, but central, and first probably to have seen afar off the rising of the waters, are the larger farmers and small squires or zemindars.

Besides these, however, who depend directly for the year's food upon the year's harvest, each in his degree, there are whole classes of others who are indirectly but vitally affected. In the villages themselves there are the fishermen and boatmen. Although actively engaged in the supply of another kind of food, these are as much concerned as their neighbours in the question of the sufficiency of the year's crop of rice. Indeed, in many cases they themselves rent and farm a patch of land.

Scattered up and down the districts, again, and in the small market-towns of the countryside there is the sprinkling of intellectuals. There are the Brahmins, or village priests; the schoolmasters; the people who have been employed on railway staffs, small stationmasters and others; clerks in village firms and shops, letter-writers, doctors, and the like. To these people the directly agricultural classes are as the very steps on which they stand, and their support being withdrawn, the flood of hunger must needs swallow them all up, the more hopelessly and inevitably since there are for them no intermediate phases of social degradation to be passed through. The peasant may perhaps, by a slow refinement of suffering, be transformed first into a landless labourer. Then, on his death or desertion, his women-folk may become gleaners, instead of proud mistresses of the farmstead. And finally, one or all of the little household may conceivably be brutalised into begging. But for a gentleman—and the village schoolmaster or doctor or small squire is perhaps *more* conscious of his pride of gentlehood than any proud belted earl in all the West!—for a gentleman, when starvation comes, there is nothing for it but to hide his head and die. Thus, over the wide stretches of green country, the river of death has risen to the height of its flood-tide, and all the prosperity and joy of the little commonwealth are gone. The hive is robbed of its honey, those spoils of hope and cheer that were gathered in the sunshine and prosperity of the good years. And how shall the spiritless bees set to work again to replace them?

III.—The Tragedy of Jute

A few sociologists, notably Professor Patrick Geddes and his school, have pointed out the necessity for studying the social significance of various agricultural and industrial products. Thus, if these men are correct, the change by a community from the manufacture of wool to that of silk for example, is not by any means so simple as would appear to the careless eye. Each different material imposes its different conditions of labour, and has in a thousand ways its own characteristic necessities. Each article produced or manufactured, therefore, will be found, according to these thinkers, if we study closely enough, to entail certain human adaptations peculiar to itself. And this we may refer to as its *social value.*

To most of us, however, this point of view has

not yet come in sight. We do not dream that there is any other standard of benefit to the worker or the consumer than the financial. And for this reason I hope to make extremely clear the story I am about to tell of Eastern Bengal.

Thirty years ago, in every cottage garden in Eastern Bengal, was found a patch more or less large as the case might be, containing a tall dark herb, botanically intermediate between a mallow and a flax, and known to us as jute.

The plant was grown by the peasants mainly for the sake of its fibre. This was very valuable in a country where rough string and bamboo are the chief building materials. There was also the supply of lamp-wicks to be thought of for the year. The leaves of the plant, moreover, when dried, were medicinal. And finally, in the case of the Hindu at home at any rate, it could not be dispensed with, since it was required in certain of the year's religious festivals. Only last year I remember, on the night of our beautiful Eastern Feast of Lamps as I went out through the lanes of our neighbourhood, being suddenly startled by a quaint little gathering of unknown objects lying on the roadway in the middle of an awkward twist in a narrow street. A light, not yet out, and a little smouldering straw, showed that I had come upon some altar of worship, and I turned to my companion for an explanation. The lad who was with me smiled easily and said: "Oh this is the *A-lakkhi puja*. It is written that on this night in 'some bad place,' with jute sticks and these few things, we should worship the Power that shines through the Unluck." Strange predestination surely: through these several centuries has Hinduism been worshipping the Unluck under the symbol of jute sticks!

The plant was open to the objection which applies also in the case of Irish flax, namely, that the long stems had to be cut down, placed in water, and practically rotted, in order to get at the fibre, and this must always have made it an aversion to the Hindu. Still its economic value and the requirements of the faith were both imperative, and the quantity grown by each cottager was only such as he and his family would consume in the year.

About some twenty to twenty-five years ago, however—owing to what chain of events I do not know, for I have not traced out the history of jute as a commercial product—it seems to have been discovered by the outside world, and its value as a fibre must have been rapidly recognised. It has the advantage, as we all now know, of being easily woven into any one of a number of attractive looking materials, some of which resemble silk and others flannel. It has the further advantage, from the modern shopkeeper's point of view, that it will not wear long, and therefore necessitates that rapid succession of garments which change of fashion is in itself only another device for bringing about. And it is further said that Bengal is the only country in the world in which it can be produced. Here then was the tragedy incipient. Twenty years ago, it is said, the cultivation of jute made its appearance on something of a commercial scale in these East Bengal districts. At first, however, it spread slowly. But some seven or eight years ago[1] it made a sudden advance, and to-day the culture of the plant is going forward by leaps and bounds. As one goes down the river from Khulna to Barisal, one sees on all hands the fields of jute alternating with the fields of rice, and this particular line of country is not as yet one of the worst infected. As one watches the boats being loaded it is always with jute, and even about Calcutta, hour after hour, day after day, the carts come pouring in along the open country roads, laden with their bales of jute. In this way the Granary of Bengal has been and is being transformed into one vast jute plantation. The temptation to the peasant was, what it always is everywhere, recklessness as to the future in the face of a large financial reward, for jute at present brings him a good price. In the

[1] This was written in 1906.

same way, as we all know, the peasants of Norway have denuded their beautiful mountains in many cases of their forests, careless always of the interests of the future, in face of that crushing need of the present which is the curse of the modern and especially of the poorer world. And in East Bengal the discovery of jute coincided with that other process by which the Commonwealth based upon Rice was being transformed inevitably into the Commonwealth based upon Money.

Such was the temptation, but in fact the bribe was a delusive one. For jute requires, for its successful culture, practically the same fields which are most favourable to rice. Thus the two crops cannot well be grown in rotation, since the soil will not afterwards produce such good rice, if, indeed, any. Besides, as we know, though the peasant cannot, the high prices will no longer be available when the growth is once universally established.

This then is what has made the present situation so hopeless. It is not only that there is no rice in the village. But far off, in lands from which the village might have drawn a supply, or at least from which some place accessible to it might have done so, there is no rice either. For these last few years, with increasing speed, all alike have been abandoning the old ideal of the conserving of rice in favour of the new wealth-producer of the hour. Till to-day, even when relief was to be brought, there was nowhere from which to bring it but distant Rangoon.

Thus the mysterious prescience of ancient faiths is justified. When the Roman Empire was but young, it may be, the simple peasants of the Gangetic Delta already worshipped the Power in the Unluck under the strangely-chosen symbol of the jute-herb, and to-day an Arctic winter of starvation has spread its mantle over them, largely through the agency of this old-time acquaintance. But what are we to say, we others, who by our greed and luxury have written so many chapters in the Martyrdom of Man, as indigo, opium, india-rubber, and now jute?

THE NORTHERN PILGRIMAGE[1]

To Indians themselves, if they have never before been on pilgrimage, the life of the pilgrim-roads is likely to be a revelation. Who uttered a doubt that India had a place and a life for women? Certainly none who had ever seen a pilgrimage. Marching along we meet them, singly or in couples, or maybe in long strings of tens and twenties, old and young mingled together. There is neither fear nor exaggerated shyness in their demeanour. Sometimes one will be separated by a few yards from her party, telling her beads, or lost in solitary thought. Sometimes, again, we meet an old woman who seems to belong to none. But almost everyone is cheerful, and almost all, from the custom of wearing their jewels all the time, have an air of festivity and brightness. All pilgrims know one another. Here none of the stiffness of a meaner world prevails. We all speak to one another as we pass. *Jai! Kedar Nath Swami ki Jai!* or *Jai! Badri Bissal lal ki Jai!* we say to each whom we meet, whether man or woman. And no words can describe the flash of sweetness

[1] See note, p. 207.

and brightness that lights up the reply. We are all out on a holiday together, and an air of gentle innocence and hilarity prevails in face of difficulties and creates a sort of freemasonry amongst all who seek the common goal. One has the chance here of studying the refinement of Eastern salutations. Sometimes a wayfarer passes who is telling her beads, or who, for some reason or another, does not care to break her silence: but oh, the dignity and charm of the bow that answers the pilgrim's salutation in such a case! Even here, in an environment which is in some ways one of intensified practicality, we meet now and again with the inveterate dreamer, living in that world upon whose shores no wave can break. It was turning into the wedge-shaped ravine of Garurganga that we came upon one such. She was a little old woman, and we caught her just as she had stepped out of her prim little shoes, placed neatly behind her, and with rapt look prostrated herself. Two people who were coming forward drew back at this, that she might not know herself interrupted, and then as again we stepped forward and came face to face with her, we saw that for the moment she was lost in the world of her own reverence. In her eyes was the look of one who saw not the earth. It was a sudden glimpse of the snow mountains to which she had paid involuntary homage.

Climbing over some peculiarly difficult boulders in the dry bed of a torrent, we met two old women, both almost blind, and bent half-double with age and infirmity. They were coming back from Badri Narayan. The place was terrible, and as we came up to them one of them stumbled. But to an ejaculation of concern, they replied, between themselves, with an air of triumph in their gaiety, "What! Is not Narayan leading? And since He has given *darsana*, what does this matter?"

I.—Hardwar and Hrishikesh

Happy they whose pilgrimage can begin at Hardwar! Never surely was there a place so beautiful. It is like Benares on a very small scale. But as one of our party remarked, people go to Benares to die, and to Hardwar as the beginning of a high undertaking. This of itself confers on the town an air of brightness. In the moonlight nights the *jatris* set out with their *pandas*, singing, as they go, along the roads. And oh, the evening worship of the Ganges! In the very middle of the lowest step of the semicircular *ghâts* of the Brahma Kund a priest stands waving what looks like a small brass tree of flame. Behind him crowd the worshippers, chiefly women, and on the bridge and island that stretch across the little bay in front of him, forming the chord of the semicircle, stand and sit other worshippers, obviously, to judge by differences of dress and type, travellers from many and various provinces. All is rapt silence while the public worship is proceeding, but as it ends the whole multitude breaks out into chanting. Choir upon choir they sing the glories of the Ganges, answering each other in the manner of an antiphon. And away beyond them stretch green islands and wooded heights, about which the blue veil of the evening mists has just begun to fall. The very scene in itself is the perfection of praise. "O ye mountains and hills, bless ye the Lord! Praise Him and magnify Him for ever! O ye rivers and streams, bless ye the Lord! Praise Him and magnify Him for ever!"

It is the railway, we are told, that has popularised Hardwar. Until a few years ago, Kankhal had been long the recognised centre, and people made pilgrimage only to Hardwar for bathing and praying, being exceedingly careful to be back before nightfall, so probable was the experience of a tiger on the road between the two places. But the fact that the habit of pilgrimage could persist at all under such circumstances is eloquent testimony to the age of the place. Kankhal itself, a couple of miles away, is the seat of Shiva as Daksheshwar, and therefore, we cannot doubt, one of the most ancient sites of Hinduism. Here we are shown the very place where Sati fell, and that where Daksha offered sacrifice. Suddenly a whole chapter of pre-Hindu Hinduism—perhaps ages long—becomes visible to us. We see that there was a time when people were familiar with the image of the goat-headed Lord of Creation. We remember the Great God Pan of the Greeks, with his one goat-foot. And we do not wonder that there should have been a struggle between this old nature-god Daksha, who may have been a personification of the Polar Star, and the new Shiva, Lord of the consciences of men.

Hrishikesh, twelve miles away from Hardwar, is a university of an ancient type. Here, amongst some of the most beautiful scenery of the Himalayas, just at the rapids of the Ganges, are hundreds of straw huts in which live *sadhus*. Amongst these it is doubtless possible to realise the ideal of the Vedic *ashramas*, in a life of simplicity, order, and learning. The first duty of the new arrival is, as I have heard, to build his own hut. Within, these men live alone or in couples, according to the merciful custom that usually carries the begging friars forth, not alone, but by twos. But when evening comes, at any rate in the winter, the great meditation fires are lighted here and there, in the open air, and seated round them the monks discourse "of settled things."

Then they relapse by degrees into the depths of thought, and when darkness has fallen and all is quiet, one after another each man slips quietly away to his own hut. It is an extraordinary combination of freedom and society, of the ideals of the hermitage and of the monastery. It may be that it gives us a glimpse of the monastic conditions of the Thebaid, but in modern times it could certainly be paralleled nowhere outside India. The *sadabratas* in the little town close by are another institution corresponding to nothing in foreign countries. Here the *sadhus* daily receive their rations of food, some cooked and some uncooked. For it is a mistake to think that those who have taken up the life of the *sannyasin* can study and think without a certain amount of bodily nourishment. Our selfishness may make us eager to preach such an ideal, but it will always be for *others* to realise! At the same time the *sadabratas* relieve the monks of the dishonour of becoming beggars, and the community of the scandal of a disorderly burden. These, in their present high organisation and development, owe a great deal to the life and work of Kambliwálá Bábá, one of the national heroes whose name is known too little outside monastic ranks. By his labours the Northern Pilgrimage has been rendered available for the thousands of pilgrims who now pass along it, and it is to be hoped that in the movement now going on for the recovery of biographies, his will not be forgotten. The present road from Hardwar to Hrishikesh, with its new temple and bazaar of Satya Narayan, is of Kambliwálá Bábá's making, as are all the good *dharmsalas* along the road. The old way to Hrishikesh lay along the Ganges-bank. In the desert-like country about Hrishikesh, one of the characteristic charities is the little water-and-mat stations, where a *gerua*-turbaned servant lives in a little hut, serving out water to each passer-by who asks for it, and keeping a clean space swept where anyone can lie down on a mat in the shade of a tree.

How old is Hrishikesh? In its very nature it is impermanent. The materials of which it is built this winter will not remain after next summer's rains. And how long the site has been used in this way, who shall say? Maybe the history of Hardwar would give us some clue to this. Maybe the *Kumbh Mela* would help us to calculate its age. The very fleetingness of its buildings must have lengthened its days, for political convulsions that would sweep clean the caves of Ajanta or Ellora would leave this winter-resort of the learned and pious entirely unaffected. As the waters of a lake close over a stone, so would Hrishikesh recover from catastrophe and grow out of its very memory. And the tradition goes, we must remember, that one of the earliest literary undertakings of the people—the division of the Vedas by Vyasa into four—was carried out in this place.

II.—SRINAGAR

We reached Srinagar five days after leaving Hardwar. The present town stands near the centre of a wide flat vale, in which the cactus and the *bo*-tree proclaim a sub-tropical climate. It is obviously new, having been rebuilt on a slightly different site so lately as the time of the Gohonna flood about fifteen years ago. This event was a great epoch-maker throughout the valleys leading up to Badri Narayan. It swept away ancient temples and images, and necessitated the re-building of many a town and village. One cannot but mourn the loss of historic remains of priceless interest, but at the same time one suspects that, from a sanitary and cleansing point of view, the flood may have done more good than harm. Like the great fire of London in 1666, it seems to have wiped out the past and banished disease-germs as well as carvings.

Srinagar has been rebuilt, as already said, since the flood, but the site of the older city is still evident enough, as one enters from the south, by the clustering of temples and shrines among the cactus hedges and peepul-trees of the wide open plain. There are many still older temples to be seen from the road, of a ponderous and severe beauty, in a type immediately preceding that of mediæval Orissa. They are comparatively small but marvellously perfect. The style must have persisted long in the Himalayas. There are examples of it, in more developed and slender form, here at Srinagar, as modern as two hundred years old; but the earliest examples must be very old indeed, dating from the days of the Hindu Revival under the Guptas, that is to say from about A.D. 400 or even earlier. Even the town of Srinagar, as it was at the time of the flood, was only founded, it is said, by Raja Ajaipal in the year 1446, so that it could not be regarded as old from an Indian point of view. But the fact is there must always have been a city here, ever since the Himalayas began to be inhabited, and certainly ever since the coming of the Asokan missions.

The geographical situation, in the midst of a valley that is almost a plain, forces the formation of an organic centre. The height is only about sixteen hundred feet above the sea, so it supports a sub-tropical vegetation and at the same time is accessible to all the cooler airs of the higher mountains. We can well imagine how the first colony of Buddhistic monks would gradually settle down, and live their monastic life, with its regular worship, preaching, and study, contented in the main to become an organic part of the life about them. Actual traces of their occupation have all been obliterated long long ago, but wherever we find a very old religious dedication, which has been a sheet-anchor of worship for century after century, we may infer with some certainty that it was established by them. Such centres exist at Srinagar in the Temples of Komoleswar and of the Five Pandavas. Of the two, Komoleswar is probably the older. The story told in the Puranas of the Mother, is here appropriated to Shiva, and he appears as the god to whom Rama made the offering of blue lotuses. There is a Shiva here of pre-Sankaracharyan type, and the temple stands in a large and ancient enclosure round which are houses and other buildings. Vaishnavism also has flowed over Komoleswar in its time, for there are scores of votive tablets carved with the feet of the Lord. But the place has never forgotten its Shaivite origin, and claims to have been visited by Sankaracharya, which we should certainly expect to have been the case. The old temple of the Five Pandavas stands on the roadway into Srinagar.

Was there once an intention of laying out the whole country with temples dedicated in order to the heroes and *munis* of the national epic? One shrinks from the thought of a task so gigantic, but there seems some reason to think it may have been contemplated, and the fact that most of these must since have disappeared is no real argument against it. The Himalayan kingdom has always been in such vital contact with the Hinduism of the plains, through *sadhus* and pilgrims and merchants, that it has shared to the full in each period as it rose, and each wave has been followed by another striving to efface the traces of that which preceded it. In this particular temple of the Five Pandavas, the Vaishnavism of Ramanuja has left its mark. There is a grotesque image of Narada worshipped here which is said to commemorate the primeval *swayambara*, where Narayana chose Lakshmi to be his spouse. The bride shrank from the appearance of Narada, who sat immediately in front of his master, and looked at Narayana himself instead. This was indeed the end to be attained, for she was the destined bride of God. But the method involved a wound to Narada's self-love, and for this he cursed Vishnu—the devotee cursed God!—saying that in a future birth as Rama he would have trouble with this wife. This is evidently a late and corrupt tale, intended to appropriate an image said to be Narada's, and to synthetise all the developments through which Vaishnavism had already passed, claiming them as historic phases of the mediæval form preached by Ramanuja.

Vaishnavism made a strong impression at Srinagar. It seems to have been held meritorious to make a pilgrimage there, and give offerings at the shrine of Lakshmi-Narayan, in lieu of going all the way to Badri Narayan. There is one grand old temple erected for this purpose four hundred years ago. Unfortunately it is now surrounded by a cactus-hedge, and is therefore inaccessible. It was superseded two hundred years later by a building of much poorer architecture. But the traditions are interesting. The Garur in front of the later temple is believed to be inferior to that which originally stood there. This, it is said, was so beautiful that it flew away! "Even this," the guide will add, with pardonable pride in local gods, "is such as you will not often see." Alas, I could not share his high opinion of the present Garur as a work of art.

There have been many Srinagars, and one of them at least would seem to have been connected with the consecration of a great rock altar to Devi. If the tradition is to be trusted, human sacrifice was practised here, and there is a story of the splendid indignation of Sankaracharya, who hurled the stone of sacrifice upside down into the river, and left to the sight of future generations only its bottom. If that was so, Sankaracharya would appear not only as the enemy of Tantrikism, but also as the reformer of Mother-worship in this matter. The rock is some miles out of the present town, and stands near a great deodar cedar on the opposite bank.

III.—Kedar Nath

The final stage of the road to Kedar Nath is terrible, especially the last four miles of steep ascent. About the beauty of the scenery one could not say enough, but the difficulties of the climb ought not to be forgotten. It is a dolorous stairway, as hard as life itself; in very truth, as the *panda* ruefully said to me, "the way to Heaven!" All this is forgotten, however, when at last we reach the uplands and begin to feel ourselves within measurable distance of Kedar Nath. We are now amongst the wide turf-covered table-lands, and the flowers begin to abound, as in some paradise of Moghul painters. At every step we pass or are passed by other pilgrims. The eagerness round and about us is indescribable. Then comes the moment when the temple is visible for the first time. A shout goes up from our carriers and others, and many prostrate themselves. We press forward more rapidly than before. It is even now a mile or so to the village. But at last we arrive, and entering find that the shrine itself stands at the end of the long avenue-like street, with the mountain and glacier rising sheer behind it, as if all India converged upon Kedar Nath as its northern point, and all roads met at the sacred feet of the Lord of Mountains. Probably, when first the temple was built in this spot, it was actually on the edge of the glacier, which in all these centuries has retreated only to a distance of less than a mile. We had made great efforts to reach our goal on a Monday, for this is held a great benison in visiting a shrine of Shiva. But when we arrived it was the middle of the day, and the temple was closed till the evening *arati*. As the afternoon ended, the cold blue mists came down from the mountains, enwrapping everything; and one sat out in the village street, watching cowled forms, in their brown *kombols*, pacing back and forth through the mist before the tight-shut doors. Suddenly we were called to see the *arati*. Darkness had fallen but the mists had gone, and the stars and the snows were clear and bright. Lights were blazing and bells clanging within the temple and we stood without, among the watching people. As the lights ceased to swing and the *arati* ended, a shout of rapture went up from the waiting crowd. Then the cry went out to clear the road, and the rush of the pilgrims up the steep steps began. What a sight was this! On and on, up and up, they came, crowding, breathless, almost struggling, in their mad anxiety to enter the shrine, reach the image, and at the last, by way of worship, to bend forward and touch with the heart the sacred point of the mountain! For this half-embrace is what the worship consists of at Kedar Nath. They poured in at the great south door, out by the east. On and on, up and up; one had not dreamed the place contained so many people as now panted forward to obtain entrance. Suddenly, from one of the doorkeepers I heard an exclamation of pity, and then he stooped and tenderly lifted a little bent old woman, bowed down under the weight of years, who had lost her footing in the crowd and might have fallen and been trodden under foot. It was one of the sights of a lifetime to stand there, in the black darkness at the top of the steps, and watch the pilgrims streaming in. It seemed as if all India lay stretched before one, and Kedar Nath were its apex, while from all parts everywhere, by every road, one could see the people streaming onward, battling forward, climbing their way up, all for what?—for nothing else than to touch God!

We had a wonderful walk next day, to the glaciers and the heights, and some of us rested on a hillside, listening to the perpetual muffled boom of the avalanches, as they broke and fell from some part or other of the great ice-mass to the north. "Yes," said the peasant who guided us, thoughtfully, as he stood gazing with us at the glacier. "It looks as if it stood perfectly still. But really it is moving, like any other river." The great temple looked small and distant now, like a village-church, and only the towering heights seemed grand enough for the worship of God. We felt this still more when we stood and looked up at the vast snowy expanse that they call the Mahaprasthan, the Great Release. For the Pandava story culminates at Kedar Nath, and we are shown the very road by which Yudhisthira and his brothers and the Lady Draupadi went, on that last great journey by which they reached the end. Others since then have followed them, it is said, and have signed their names at the last on a great rock-face that stands on the way. We made our way there: and sure enough we found numbers of trisuls drawn in white and black and red, in wavering lines some of them, as if by hands that shook with age, and some of them strong and firm: but all, if the country-folk are to be believed, the autographs of those who felt that desire was ended and the supreme renunciation now theirs to make. For the *Shastras*, say those who know, make man free of society at two places, Kedar Nath and Allahabad.

The site of Kedar Nath is very old. There is

a temple of Satya-Narayana built over a spring, in the village-street. There is also a tiny chapel containing the nine forms of Devi. There are pre-Sankaracharyan Shivas also, and square water-courses, dotted about the central shrine. On the whole it would seem as if, at the period commonly referred to as the visit of Sankaracharya, Satya-Narayana had been superseded by Shiva as the principal deity. And the Devi-worship which was probably still older than Satya-Narayana remained henceforth side by side with it, in a similar subordination. The question of the order in which its pre-Sankaracharyan phases succeeded one another is the great crux of the story of Hinduism.

The carving round the doorway of the temple is evidently ancient, and the ornament consists of Hinduistic figures of gods and kings contained in niches, not unlike those which contain Buddhas in the last of the art-periods at Ajanta. This would predispose us to assign a date between the expulsion from Gandhara, A.D. 751, and the year 1000, leaning somewhat to the latter because of the very manifest decadence in style. We must remember that the importance of Kedar Nath as a place of pilgrimage has always kept it in touch with the plains, and that at the same time there seems never to have been any Mohammedan invasion of these Himalayan valleys. These facts explain why it is possible to find in this remote spot an important link between older Buddhistic and later Hindu sculpture.

Above all, Kedar Nath is the shrine of the *sadhus*. As in the days of Buddhism, so in those of Sankaracharya, and as then so also now, the yellow robe gleams and glistens in all directions. There is no begging, for the *sada-bratas* supply all the wants of monastic visitors. But there is a world of enthusiasm, and still the tradition goes amongst them that Kedar Nath is a place of good omen for *sannyasins*, for here came Sankaracharya and falling into *samadhi* died.

It was the second day of our stay when an old man who had been seriously ill for many months reached the place and made his *darsana*. He had ended his journey, and hastened to fulfil his vow within the hour. But scarcely had he done so, barely had he ceased from prayer, not yet was the rapture of achievement abated, when the battle was declared for him to be finished, and in the bright morning air, with long sighing breaths, his soul went forth. Such is the benediction with which the Lord of Mountains lays His hand upon His own!

NOTE TO THE NORTHERN PILGRIMAGE

When we consider the overwhelming import of the Himalayan range to the people inhabiting the plains of Northern India, it is not surprising that the Hindus should, from time immemorial, have looked upon the snow-capped peaks as the Abode of the Gods and have deified the rivers which take their rise among them. The slopes of the Himalayas and the banks of the rivers along their upper courses were dotted in past ages with hermitages, monasteries, and colleges, which were the spring-heads of Indian civilisation and spirituality. A few of these still exist, while the shrines that are visited by multitudes of pious pilgrims are very numerous and of a sanctity unsurpassed. The most famous are Mount Kailas, Lake Manasa Sarovara, Kedar Nath, Badri Narayan, Hrishikesh, Hardwar, and Amarnath. The last-named (in Kashmir) was visited by Sister Nivedita in company with the Swami Vivekananda, and is the subject of a chapter in *The Web of Indian Life*. The pilgrimage here described is that to the group of sacred places situated in the Kumaon division of the United Provinces.

Hardwar is one of the seven holy places spoken of in the Puranas as especially leading to *Moksha*, salvation. The town stands on the right bank of the Ganges, close by the gorge through which the sacred river debouches on to the plains. It is the scene, every twelfth year, of a vast assemblage of pilgrims, on the occasion of the *Kumbh Mela*.

Hrishikesh is distinguished among holy places by reason of the fact that it has preserved intact its character as a hermitage and place of learning. Hindu ascetics still live there in thatched huts, sleeping on grass-mats, content with the barest necessities obtained by begging, speaking little or not at all, making spiritual culture and the pursuit of divine knowledge their sole concern.

Srinagar, a principal town of the Garhwal district, is of course to be distinguished from the city of the same name in Kashmir. It stands on the left bank of the Alaknanda, the head stream of the Ganges, and owes its importance to its position on the pilgrim route. The old town was washed away in 1894, by a flood caused through the bursting of the Gohnā Lake.

Kedar Nath, immediately below the snow-peak of Mahāpanth, at an elevation of 11,753 feet, marks the spot where Shiva, in his flight from the Pandavas, assumed the form of a buffalo and dived into the earth, leaving his hind-quarters on the surface. Four miles from the temple, on the way to the Mahāpanth peak, is the precipice known as the Bhairab Jhāmp, whence sometimes the devotee, in the ecstasy of attainment, would fling himself down.

The shrine of Badri Narayan is below the peak of Badrinath (23,210 feet). It stands on a shoulder of the mountain, at an elevation of 10,400 feet, on the road from Srinagar to the Mana Pass. Tradition points to Sankaracharya as the founder of the original temple.

THE SHIP OF FLOWERS

It is empty now, the place on my desk where the little ship of flowers has stood all day. But out on the chill edge of the Ganges, as darkness comes on, the tiny bark lies drifting, hither and thither, scarcely determined betwixt ebb and flow, as we with a few of the children launched it an hour ago. It was early still when we went down to the riverside, and as we turned away only one worshipper had arrived besides ourselves—a solitary girl of eleven or twelve—to send her offering out to the Great Unknown. We stayed awhile then and watched her, as she carefully removed the sacramental food from the birch-bark vessel, set in the stern the little light, and then floated it boldly out upon the waters. And after that, what could we do but stay and watch and watch, with breathless interest, as long as ever the star shone clear in the fragile craft which, we knew, with the turn of the tide, would reach the main current and be carried far out to sea? O! innumerable fleet of little nameless boats, floating on ponds and rivers, in all the villages of Bengal to-night, each bearing its twinkling lamp into the all-enshrouding dark, how like ye are to life, how like to death!

For this is the last day of the Bengal month of *Pous*. It is the old-time day for pilgrimage to Ganga-Sagar—that island where the river meets the sea. And more than this, it is the day of prayer for all travellers, all wanderers from their homes, for all whose footsteps at nightfall shall not lead to their own door. It was in a crowded street this morning, as I passed the end of a small bazaar, that I noticed the eager faces and hurrying feet of men and women, hastening to carry to those at home the ships of flowers. They were rude enough, these little ships, that I too bought, to load with spoil of loving thought. Roughly pinned together they were, made of the shining white core of the plantain-stalk, and masted and arched from stem to stern with splinters of bamboo, run through the hearts of yellow marigolds. Here and there the dealers had made feint to imitate more closely, with coloured paper flags and string, the sails and cordage of the old country boats. But for the most part they were mere suggestions, glistening vessel and burning-hearted flowers.

Mere suggestions, truly—but of what! Can we not see the quiet women, sitting absorbed before the symbol at their feet, loading it with offerings

—*bel*-leaves, flowers, the consecrated fruits and grain, and praying with each fresh gift for some beloved life, that through the coming year it might go safe amidst whatever tide, that even now, if peril somewhere threaten it, it may be led safe home? Have we not here to-day the perfect picture of Humanity—Man battling on the distant frontier-line of toilsome life; and Woman—for love's sake, not for God's—holding fast to prayer?

One thinks of the cry of the Jew, sonorous through the ages—the Jew, who loved not the sea, but lifted his eyes to the hills, to find his help, and lost himself, between "I" and "thee," in an inflood of blessedness: "The Lord shall preserve thy going out and thy coming in, from this time forth, and even for evermore." One thinks of the churches of Brittany, and the small model of a ship, *barque de ma vie*, that hangs before every altar and in every private oratory. And there comes back the echo of the sailor's cry, amid surf and storm, *Sainte Anne! Sainte Anne!*

Here too, in Bengal, we have a maritime people, once great among the world's seafarers, and here, on the last day of *Pous*, we celebrate the opening of the annual commercial season, the old-time going forth of merchant enterprise and exploration. It was a traffic cut off from that of Phœnicia, and all the well-omened peoples of the Middle Sea, but unmistakably great in the East. China and Japan, Cambodia and Burma, have welcomed the coming of the Bengal mariners to their ports, being glad to win honour and wealth thereby. Fa Hian, Hiouen-Tsang, and I-Ching are but three names, out of countless hosts to whom they belonged, who sought the shores of India, or left them, in the name of the knowledge and impulse that she had power to send to other and less favoured peoples. But why cast our memory so far back? It is little more than a hundred years since Indian shipbuilding was famous through the world. Even now the wooden shipping that still plies between the small countries of north-western Europe is in great part discarded craft of Indian building and of Indian teak. And how should these eastern vessels have won renown if the merchants and sailors of India had not been great to man and use?

All day long, from the altar-shelf above my desk, the marigolds, like an arch of sanctuary-lamps, have shone down upon me, and stirred a maze, a multitude, of dreams and memories in heart and brain. "The Lord bless—the Lord bless—going out—coming in—even for evermore!" Do we not stand, even as here, on the river shores of life, and watch the going forth of beloved souls into the perils of the world's high seas, yea, into the far space and mystery of death?

Yet hold we by that very light, so like a star, they carry at-their prow, that how distant soever be the journey set, they shall not pass beyond the reach of this our love and prayer, nor break outside the encircling barriers of the heart of God.

THE END